The Real
GOOD NEWS
from
GOD

EARL CAMPBELL

The Real Good News From God

by Earl Campbell
Lettra Press

book review by Barbara Bamberger Scott

"The purpose of God is life eternal with an abundance of living things all praising and giving glory to the eternal God, Yahweh."

Drawing heavily on the Bible, author Campbell expresses his strong conviction that the world as we know it today is under the domination of Satan and his forces. Still, this reign of evil will end, and a new earth will emerge, as predicted and planned from the beginning. One basic tenet presented is that everything is composed of three parts, including the universes themselves: the infinite, the metaphysical, and the physical. Campbell wishes to correct errors that many Christians assume to be true. One such error concerns the notion of heaven and hell. He asserts that all who die are in a dreamless state of unconsciousness, awaiting the final judgment. Campbell demonstrates how these erroneous ideas evolved by arraying biblical quotations in correct perspective and fine detail, addressing such issues as the truth of a worldwide flood and the existence of giants before it. He concludes that the new earth, God's kingdom, will arise after the war of Armageddon, which appears to be occurring today.

Campbell constructs his various theses with intelligent organization and an apparent zeal to share biblical facts with those who the misrepresentations of some religious sects have lulled. He decries most world religionsâ Islam, Buddhism, and certain Christian groupsâ except for the one that gave him what he sees as the true perspective: Jehovah's Christian Witnesses, who refuse to engage in the "immoral practices of the modern world." He urgently advises readers to become aware of the signs of the imminent restoration of the earth and the destruction of Satan and his followers. Above all, he passionately urges people to follow a righteous pathway so that they may share in this glorious, promised end time. Campbell's evident conviction and sincerity give his material credence, especially for those who share his view and those approaching it for the first time.

THE ONLY WAY TO ETERNAL LIFE !

This Extraordinary Book has been written and now published for the Sole Purpose of guiding all of humanity to the One REAL TRUTH that leads to Eternal Life And True Happiness !

There are Only 2 Roads Involved (Matthew 7:13,14) Here Is A description Of Them And Where They Lead To !

THE NARROW ROAD: This Is The road That Leads One To Eternal Life It is Reserved Only for those of Humankind Who Have shown By Their Actions. In Life Where They Have Taught Themselves To Love God And Have Come To Realize and Discovered That The best Way To Be Happy Has been To Follow The Laws Of God And Really Apply Them On A Daily Basis In Their Every day Lives, And To Follow The Perfect Example Of The Savior, Jesus Christ Who Provided The One True Way To Eternal Life By Giving Up His " Perfect Life" For All Of The Sins Of Humankind, and so made a way out of imperfection to All Those who Accept This Free Gift Of God And Who Show This By How They Live Their lives In Harmony With The Laws Of God For Those Who Are To Inherit Eternal Life In A Paradise Earth That Is About To Come Under The Rulership Of " THE KINGDOM OF GOD " And Is To Last For 1000 Years Under Jesus !

THE BROAD ROAD: This Is The Road That Leads To Eternal Everlasting Cutting Off From Life That Has Unfortunately Been The Road Chosen By The Majority Of Humankind To Follow. It Is The Way Of The World That Is At Enmity With The True God As Jesus Stated, and All Those Who Continue On This Road Are Destined For Everlasting Cutting Off From Life In The Second Death That Is Symbolized By Gehenna, The " Lake Of Fire " In The Final Judgement. See These Texts In ... Revelation 20: 11-14 and MATTHEW 25 : 46 as to what happens to All Of the Wicked ones 1 They have chosen to ignore the laws of the Creator of The Universe and to follow the ways of the world instead that is governed by the great satan who is deceiving the entire world of mankind into beleiving his many lies including the many false religions with their many different beliefs that have been used to divide the peoples of earth and have been responsible for many of the conflicts that have taken so many lives. over the centuries !

ASK YOURSELF THIS QUESTION ?

Which Road Have you Been On ?

Let The Lord Jesus Show You The Way Where He States

. . . "I AM The Way - The Truth - And The Life"

No One Comes To The father Except Through Me !!!

Please Read These two texts in The Bible at 1 John 4: 6-14 and Acts 4 : 12

Copyright © 2021 by Earl Campbell.

All rights reserved. No part of this book may be reproduced, transmitted, or distributed in any form by any means, including, but not limited to, recording, photocopying, or taking screenshots of parts of the book, without prior written permission from the author or the publisher. Brief quotations for noncommercial purposes, such as book reviews, permitted by Fair Use of the U.S. Copyright Law, are allowed without written permissions, as long as such quotations do not cause damage to the book's commercial value. For permissions, write to the publisher, whose address is stated below.

Printed in the United States of America.

ISBN   978-1-953150-82-0   (Paperback)
ISBN   978-1-953150-83-7   (Digital)

Lettra Press books may be ordered through booksellers or by contacting: Lettra Press LLC
30 N Gould St. Suite 4753 Sheridan, WY 82801
1 307-200-3414 | info@lettrapress.com www.lettrapress.com

ABOUT THE AUTHOR

I was born into this world in 1934 to a family who already consisted of 4 sisters and an older brother, as well as a father who was a school teacher and poet, who professed that he was an athiest, and so we never had any religion in the family that I was ever aware of. I always felt that it was rather odd that God was always included in his many poetry writings that were never published however. I still have many of his works in a number of his notebooks.

I found that narrow path that leads to eternal life in a very strange way that began one evening while having dinner at one of my younger brothers place, where I had gotten into a religious discussion with my brothers wife about the man Jesus, who she did not believe that he was the Son of God, but merely just a man, a prophet, but not the Savior of the world of mankind.

I remember answering her by the following statement, and I did not know until that moment how deeply that I believed that Jesus was exactly who he had claimed to be, as I blurted out the following comment, and I quote, "If I believed as you do, I would shoot myself tonight and end it all right now"! I had never discussed religion with anyone until that very night, and here is where it gets very strange indeed, because within the very next week, I was contacted by two different religions, first came two young mormon missionaries, who I had never been contacted by before as I had never seen or talked to any religious people before. Next came two of Jehovah's Witnesses in the same week. They offered to answer the many questions that I had about many, many things, and so I agreed to have them come back again the following week, and so I started on the path of understanding the real truth about what the Bible really says about many things, and which I have found to be totally contrary to what the world of mankind have been taught to believe by the many different religions including the many differing beliefs of the churches of christendom.

This is the main reason for my publishing this extraordinary Book, and to help still others to find that narrow path that leads to eternal life. Please read this text in a Bible at Matthew 7:7-14; 21-23 The most high God waits for each one of us to ask of him the way to eternal life. Matthew 7:7,8

P.S. I have no doubt that the words I spoke that night long ago were heard by the angels of GOD !

AN INTRODUCTION TO THE MYSTERIES OF THE AGES AND GOD THE CREATOR OF ALL THINGS

The main purpose of this book is to help mankind understand some of the mysteries that have plagued humans since the beginning of time and the creation of intelligent and inquisitive minds that have wondered about many things as to who or what created mankind and the universe, a good question that no one has been able to answer until now and one that this book intends to answer, including many other mysteries!

For example, was there ever a worldwide flood that covered the entire planet? If so, where is the evidence? This book will do just that in supplying the evidence, along with indisputable facts that are undeniable, including some 277 accounts of a flood from all corners of the earth, the same one mentioned in the Bible in the book of Genesis 6 and which is corroborated by several other people, including Jesus and the apostles Peter and Paul. (Matthew 24:37–39; Hebrews 11:7; 2 Peter 3:5, 6; and Luke 17:27)

There is much physical evidence all over the earth in a variety of locations, such as beached whale skeletons in sand graves in the Sahara Desert far from the sea and other giant mammoths frozen in ice with green tropical vegetation in their mouths and stomachs, suggesting that they were quickly frozen, which would only happen if the atmosphere around the planet suddenly grew much thinner, especially where these were found in Siberia.

The many other mysteries on this planet, such as the Stonehenge, the Pyramids of Egypt, and the Giant Statues on Easter Island, as well as giant monuments in many locations all over the earth, will be answered in the pages of this book and we hope to the satisfaction of all mankind! Some of these monuments were so large and made with such precision with blocks of rock and stone weighing many tons that no one today has been able to ever explain how these ancient people were able to have created these massive structures. Please read on to discover the answers to all these many mysteries!

A FURTHER BRIEF INTRODUCTION TO THIS BOOK

Everything in GOD's universes is designed in threes, just as GOD itself is made up of three separate beings. This book, like the Bible, uses the familiar language of genders when referring to "God," the Word, "the Holy Spirit" because mankind better understands that type of analogy regarding the mystery of godliness.

In the "first infinite universe," there are three separate heavens that include God's heavenly throne, with millions of spirit beings in attendance. See 2 Corinthians 12:1–4 and Daniel 7:9, 10, just as there are a total of three separate universes.

- *THE INFINITE UNIVERSE – Containing God's throne*
- *THE METAPHYSICAL "U" – Containing spirit beings*
- *THE PHYSICAL UNIVERSE – Containing human beings*

In the very beginning of the infinite universe—before there was any form of intelligence or awareness of being and the ethers of infinity had as yet not coalesced into an awareness of being aliveness—the ethers of atomic structure over eons of cosmic time slowly acquired a semblance of individuality that led to what the Bible refers to as the great "I AM," as recorded in Exodus 3:14. "I AM" the Universe and all that it contains, I have created all that IS, and all that now exists, and all that is to come throughout eternity. "'I AM' the first and 'I AM' the last." There was no God formed before me, and there never will be any other like me. I alone created "all that is," Who was with me? See Isaiah 44:6, 24; 45:5, 12, 18, and 22.

Please read on to discover in much more detail the answers to many of the strange mysteries of the three universes and of God, itself, along with the explanations about what scientists refer to as invisible dark matter and dark energy that seem to control the physical universe by its influence on the physical world of galaxies that scientists can see, much like those other invisible forces called gravity and wind!

PREFACE OF THIS EXTRAORDINARY BOOK

There are three introductions to this extraordinary book of the explanations about GOD, JESUS CHRIST, the BIBLE, and all mankind. The real purpose of this book is to correct many of the erroneous theories of mankind and to simplify and to explain these misunderstandings that people have about the Bible and the secrets that have been hidden within its pages until now. Daniel 12:4 tells where mankind have been kept in the dark about what is about to happen, where the earth and everyone in it are about to experience a great tribulation such as the world has never had before. See Matthew 24:21–22 regarding the prophecy about that happening. The signs that Jesus foretold are all around us today.

The reason for this book is to help people understand the meaning of all these happenings that are occurring in the world and what they mean to you as an individual because of the things written in the Bible. These will be explained in detail to help people see the real truth about many different subjects. For example, when one reads in Genesis 1:26 where it states the following, and we quote, "Let US make man in OUR image," you might wonder about who GOD is talking to when he says "let US." Who is US? By going to another part of the Bible, we will show you just who GOD was talking to, as in the book of Colossians 1:15–20 as well as John 1:1–3 and 14 and Hebrews 1:1–3.

This book will explain in simple, truthful ways many of the false ideas that mankind have been misled into believing about GOD, Jesus Christ, and the Devil or Satan and just why bad things are happening to normal law-abiding people. Still, there is another example of erroneous thinking that show Jesus having LONG HAIR in many of Hollywood movies, together with other portrayals in pictures of Jesus with long hair. Let us see what the Bible says about the subject of a person having long hair, as in 1 Corinthians 11:14. It should be obvious to all that Jesus did not have long hair—as it would have been a dishonor to him, as the text makes plain!

The Bible shows that if a woman has long hair, it is a glory to her, as it is given to her instead of a headdress. So all of you men who have been wearing your hair long as a woman, you now must realize that you have been dishonoring yourself. You would think that those who are responsible for facts in a movie would at the very least try to check in the Bible for the truth, but obviously, they cannot be bothered with the truth, something one must always be concerned about when watching movies that are mostly fictional and have nothing to do with the real facts.

This book, on the other hand, is not fictional but rather is very concerned with the real truth about all subjects relating to God, the Creator, and Jesus Christ, the King of kings, and the three separate universes, as well as all mankind, the animal creation and the earth itself, and the future of everything into infinity, as well as the true meaning of words in the Bible, so that all people may have a clear understanding of what the Bible really is saying.

All these different subjects will be explained in simple, detailed ways by using Bible texts in every instance, so as to make the Bible come alive and easy to understand for everyone who wants to know the real truths that have been hidden from mankind by a world that has been designed to hide the real facts from the entire world by the great enemy of truth, Satan, the Devil, along with all his followers that have been misleading mankind by every means of deception and half truths and that have created doubts in the minds of all thinking people.

That is Satan's main objective—to cause doubt—just as he did in the Garden of Eden, when he lied to Eve. See these texts in the Bible about this subject at Ephesians 6:11–17, and 2 Corinthians 11:14, as well as Matthew 4:8–10 that shows that the Devil is the ruler of this present system of things where he is seen offering Jesus all the kingdoms of the world, if he will just bow down to him.

The Bible makes it very clear for everyone who is interested in truth as to just who the present ruler of this world of humankind is that is alienated from the true ruler of the universe that is God the Almighty. See the following texts in the Bible in John 8:23 and John 12:31 where Jesus draws a distinction between the world above that is governed by God and the world below that is ruled and governed by Satan, the Devil, and his demon followers.

See also John 14:30 and John 16:11, showing Satan, the ruler of this world, having been judged and having no power over Jesus. The Bible in many other texts show why Satan has been allowed to continue as the ruler of the present systems of things so as to try and prove that its way of ruling is the better choice for all to see and to allow each generation of mankind the opportunity to choose for themselves as to which is preferable to them! This is the main reason for God's allowance of time for the Devil's rule.

If you have ever wondered why the entire world is in such dire straits and why it has been allowed to go on this way for so long without any interference from the creator of the entire universe, then please, by all means, read on to discover all the reasons as to just why everything that has happened in the past has had a very good long-lasting purpose in God's allowance of time, not just to prove Satan. The liar that he is but the opportunity for all of you to either agree with God's way of doing things or the Devil's way. That is a choice that you have been given to make.

Please read on to enjoy all the real truths and their explanations made easy to understand from the Bible and how they all relate to you and your family and all mankind as you are all in this together with your Creator, GOD, and learn what is to happen in the very near future, as well as far into the everlasting future of GOD's ETERNAL CREATIONS (A WORLD WITHOUT END).

THE FIRST UNIVERSE

PURE GOD ENERGY

*From pure mind and unlimited energy,
the Creator GOD produced all that now exists
what some modern scientists now refer to as*

THE BIG BANG

*Which they believe was the beginning of
the physical universe that involves only
about 5 percent of the known visible universe
that humans can see; the other about 95 percent
that is unseen involves dark energy and
dark matter, which they believe controls
the visible universe by its effect that
scientists can see, much like the wind on*

*earth, an unseen force but is obvious by
its effects or that other invisible force,
gravity, that affects everything on earth!*

> (See Hebrews 11:3)
> Read on for more about GOD
> and dark energy and dark matter

THE SECOND UNIVERSE

THE METAPHYSICAL WORLD

*This invisible world, the other about 95 percent, is the world
of spirit beings that controls the world of billions of
galaxies including the earth and its sun!
(See Daniel 7:9, 10; Job 1:6; and Isaiah 45:12 and 18)*

*This is the metaphysical world of spirits,
(what humans know as angels)
This is the invisible world that scientists
believe does exist because of its influence
on the physical world and includes
about 95 percent of the known visible universe
that is invisible to the world of humankind.
This invisible part of the physical world
is referred to as dark energy and dark matter.*

THE 3 INVISIBLE FORCES THAT OPERATE IN THE PHYSICAL UNIVERSE
BLACK HOLES
DARK MATTER *DARK ENERGY*

These 3 forces that scientists refer to as dark is an erroneous description of them as they are just simply invisible to human eyes, instead of dark! This is because scientists are not aware of their true function in this physical Universe. I will explain in simple terms what the function of these 3 forces is! Dark Energy or rather invisible energy which is a more apt description is the source of energy that supplies the physical Universe giving it the ability to continue to function, and to also create new Star Systems including all their planets, moons, etc. in this " Ever Expanding Universe " without end!

Dark Matter that is also invisible to human eyes are the stuff that keeps existing matter in this Visible Universe in equilibrium, much the same as you would understand Matter and Anti-Matter or Magnetic and Anti-Magnetic forces. This matter controls all physical bodies in order to prevent them from colliding with others in this Visible Universe. BLACK HOLES as they are also just invisible to human eyes, are " The Gateways to The Meta-Physical and Invisible Universe, and what I refer to as "The RECYCLING GAS STATIONS " of the physical Universe. Their function in the simplest terms is to take in old matter and gasses, recycle it and spew it out again in vast quantities as new and invisible matter and energy with the purpose of sustaining the Physical Universe as well as allowing the creation of New Star Systems that are being created continuously in an ever-expanding Physical Universe! Each Galaxy contains at least one of these " Recycling Gas Stations "as I Jokingly refer to them as. in the simplest of terms. The Real Truth is many times quite the opposite to human scientific thinking as has been the case in millennia past so my advice to all of you. is to keep on theorizing and always seeking new and exciting answers to the many interesting things that are still to be discovered in this "Fantastic Physical Universe ". Just imagine how boring this world would be if you knew everything that there was to know, and there were no more challenges for humans to try and figure out. Only an ": All Wise GOD "could have created this Wild and Wonderful Physical Universe that is so diversified so as to keep everyone interested in life and the many challenges that we all face each and every day. It reminds one of a text in the Bible that states and I Quote, "God opens his Hands and satisfies the desire of every living thing" Psalms 146-16

So, keep on enjoying the many diversified challenges and look on them as opportunities to overcome them. That is what makes life such a wonderful experience, also always remember to give thanks to the one who made all of this wonderful Universe a reality for all of humankind to enjoy for all of eternity, without end!

P.S. Just a further explanation about the Meta-Physical Universe and its function and some of the responsibilities it has regarding the Physical Universe. The beings in this Invisible Universe are what Humans refer to as Angels. Their responsibility is to maintain the equilibrium of the Many Physical Star systems, their planets, moons, etc., They are aided in this by millions of Robotic Entities that were created to operate in the Physical Universe as helpers to the angels so as to maintain all the systems in the proper order as intended by the Creator. They have sometimes been seen by humans and are those that are described as " The Grays " with large heads and Bulbous Eyes. They use space ships of many different shapes and sizes. Some of these have also been seen by people including pilots as well as some Politicians.

Their Mother Ships are monstrous in size and are used to control and maintain Planet Orbits and moons as well as all other objects in this Physical Universe, so as to maintain order as every created thing in this Universe requires monitoring and maintenance, which includes Planets and their moons. All of the many satellites that man has been able to loft up into the upper stratosphere of the earth will eventually lose their orbital speed and begin to fall back to the earth. The created things of GOD just last a lot longer, but they too require continual monitoring and maintenance and will also eventually cease their life span. There is not a thing in this Physical Universe that lasts forever, or does not need to be changed or replaced. (Hebrews 11:11 & 12)

THE REAL TRUTH ABOUT " UFO'S

* How Are They Able To Appear And Disappear ?
* How Are They Able To Fly So Erratically ?
* How Are They Able To Travel So Fast Instantly ?

These are all very Good Questions, Are They Not ?

Here are the answers and the reasons as to why they are able to do what they have been seen doing They are not commanded by hunan entities , but instead by God's Angelic beings or their many Robotic Entity Helpers. Their responsibility is to govern all of God's many physical Creations in this Physical Universe.

They are responsible for the continual monitoring and occasional maintenance of all the Galaxies with their many Star Systems and Planets, moons, asteroids, Comets, Etc. This is why they have been seen on many occasions by humans here on earth, as they have been monitoring all happenings with regards to human activities and any dangers that could affect other systems in this Galaxy.

The Style and Size of their many different Crafts are dependent on their particular mission at the time.. Many of their craft are smaller in size because they are used to enter the earth's atmosphere more easily, where their larger Vessels remain outside of the earth's atmos phere. Some of these " Mother Ships" as they have been referred to are Gigantic in Size and are used to transfer the smaller crafts to other Star Systems many times faster than the "Speed Of Light", in an instant of time as it were.. much like the so-called " Worm Holes" that earth scientists have wondered about.

These " Mother Ships" have the power to move certain large objects including Planets and Moons back into their proper orbit if and when necessary. All Physical Creations require monitoring and Maintenance, as every physical body whether Stars , Planets or Moons, Etc. never stay still but are always moving, and just like all of Man's creations , they all need looking after.

There is also a constant observation and collection of DNA data on the evolution of different Species on earth, as God keeps records of all created thimgs. It is quite possible that it was one of these craft that crashed in the Roswell case of 1947, and very possibly the U.S Govt. may very well have some of these Robotic Entities in their possession. as all created things are susceptible to accidents or other happenings unforseen , or otherwise, even those of God's created things, just like Humans many created physical creations, Is that not the case?

So Now You Know The " REAL TRUTH " About UFO's !

<u>They are the protectors of the earth and humankind.</u>

THE REAL REASON FOR THE THIRD UNIVERSE

THE PHYSICAL UNIVERSE

Imagine if you will, a magnificent, almighty being with infinite wisdom and knowledge but as yet all alone without any intelligent beings to converse or communicate with.

What would such a being lack or desire to know about itself? It was magnificent, yes, but what does that mean? Because that word is but a relative term!

*We will use the term GOD
throughout this book because
it is a term that humans recognize
as a supernatural, all-powerful
Being with Miraculous Powers,*

THE "UNIVERSE" DIVIDED FROM THE CREATOR

In rendering the universe as a divided version of itself, God produced from PURE ENERGY all that now exists—both the unseen universe and the metaphysical one that exploded into an infinite number of units that were smaller than the whole individual spirits like their Father and Creator, Almighty God. These energy units are what humans refer to as angels and could be called God's spiritual children in this case. See 1 Corinthians 2:11 as well as 3:9, 16, 17; and Luke 8:27, 28, and 55 among many other such passages we will quote from in this book.

As children of the Supreme God, they too would possess similar qualities and creative powers that they would be able to exercise in the physical world, much like the ones that Jesus showed when he was here on earth—the many miracles that he was able to perform, such as walking on water and commanding the wind and sea to obey him (Luke 8:23–25).

THOUSANDS OF HEAVENLY ANGELS SURROUND GOD'S THRONE

*God's divine purpose in creating
other intelligent spirit beings
was so that they might share
his joy of being and aliveness
and so that it could know
itself through the actual experience
of these spirit children, and so
it gave to each the same
creative powers that God has.
All this was essential
in order to understand in
a real physical way what it is
like in the actual experience.
Notice how the Bible shows
this in the situation about
Jesus in Hebrews 2:10, 18.*

A BRIEF HISTORY OF TIME AND THE BEGINNING OF EVERYTHING

Imagine if you will go back into time, further back, and yet still further back into the swirling mists of infinity some billions of earth years to see yourself looking at the very inception of time and the very beginning of an awareness of being alive and possessing a seeming power of mind. What do you see? But vast clouds of gasses, atoms in swirling chaotic array with no semblance of order—but wait, all of a sudden, out of the mists of atoms, you see a swirling mass far larger than all the others that is attracting more of these smaller mists to itself!

This larger mass has coalesced into an awareness of being, an aliveness that is able to exert a mental power over these other atoms of gasses so as to manipulate them to do its bidding and to incorporate them into itself. What is this giant ball of gas that is doing this? This, my friends, is "the Beginning of everything" that now exists and also the future that contains all three universes that this book is going to be explaining in detail, along with an explanation of mankind that have also been evolving from primitive origins to the intelligent society of today, with all the creative talents and abilities and by the power of pure mind and thought that have been able to create all the modern conveniences that people enjoy today, including air travel, trains, automobiles, electricity, atomic power, and all the associated things that make life so enjoyable in the modern world.

Just like the first original thought that created what the Bible now refers to as GOD, the Almighty "I AM!" I AM the universe and all that it contains! "I AM the first and I AM the last!" Before me, there was no GOD formed!

Please see these texts in your Bible in John 1:1–3; Isaiah 43:10, 11; Revelation 1:8, 17, 18; 2:8. And afterward, there continued to be no other gods formed; I AM the ONLY ONE! There are no other gods like me! I alone am GOD (Isaiah 45:22 and 48:12–13). Just like the original thought that over eons of time created GOD, so over many of earth years, mankind have also evolved to the intelligent beings of today! Why is it so difficult to understand the parallel of the creation of God and mankind?

IN ORDER TO UNDERSTAND THE EVOLUTION OF GOD AND MAN ONE MUST REASON AS BELOW

In simple terms, God is the universe; and as the universe expands, so does God—as God is expanding with the entire universe as well as mankind in their own way. In the beginning, as man must—of necessity with its limited view of infinity—have a starting point of everything, we will say that there was a vast amount of dark matter and dark energy in the ethers of infinity; and in vast eons of endless time, it finally began to acquire an innate awareness of intelligence and being with the ability to influence other atoms in the ethers to create structures by the power of pure mind.

This is what the Bible refers to as the Almighty "I AM" as recorded in the book of Exodus 3:14, 15, as well as John 8:58 where Jesus claimed to be the "I AM." In other words, "I am everything, I am all things, I am the first and the last!" I am also "the three universes combined" (Isaiah 44:6, 24; 45:12, 18, 22; 46:9, 10; and 48:12, 13).

THE UNIVERSE ITSELF FIRST CREATED THE BEING KNOWN AS ALMIGHTY GOD AND THEN THE UNIVERSES

So in the most simple terms, it was the universe itself that created this intelligent being that the Bible refers to as God and further states that this being created everything else that exists through its all-powerful Word
The so-called second personage of the Almighty Triune God that we will explain in much more detail in the pages of this book. See Hebrews 1: 1–3, 8–10.

THE COSMOS CREATED THE "GOD BEING"

So once mankind can reason on the possibility that the cosmos that we know exists created an intelligence over eons of time and that being they call GOD—and as the Bible states created the physical universe by means of its powerful Word, as when GOD issues a command for something to become a reality in a physical world—it appears as if out of the ethers, as Hebrews 11:3 describes.

A PHYSICAL IMAGE OF GOD

In the Bible in John 1:14, it states that the Word of GOD became a person of flesh and blood, who the world know as JESUS, the SON of GOD, and that this one was to be called Im-man'ue-l, which means "GOD with us" in a flesh-and-blood person. It is very interesting to note how this person, Jesus, was able to perform all kinds of miracles so far as mankind were concerned—such as control over the wind and sea—or able to heal people's illnesses and diseases and even to bring persons back from the dead.

In the following texts in the Bible, Matthew 8:26 and 27 and Luke 8:24, 25, 55, Jesus was able to control the physical energy atoms in this physical world, much like when he performed the miracle of the loaves and fishes so as to feed several thousand people with just five loaves and two fishes (Mark 6:38–44; 4:39–41).

The Bible invites everyone to come and reason on all these things, as it is GOD's will for mankind to evolve into a superior intelligence so as to be able to do those same things that the Lord Jesus was able to do—at will—as he stated in several places, such as in Matthew 17:20; 21:19–22; 15:30, 31, as well as in Mark 11:20–24 and 9:17–27. So let us reason on the facts: The universe is a fact that we can see. We realize that someone or something had to have created THE BIG BANG just as every created thing has to have a creator.

THE REAL REASON FOR THE HUMAN FAMILY

God's purpose in creating the human family with the ability to procreate themselves was so that God might know itself, as God through the eyes and experiences of humans as well as in the spiritual realm. There was no other way to do this except through real physical people. God's purpose for humans is for them to know themselves as part of God and to recall who they really are and where they have come from as individual parts of their creator. The Bible states this in real terms where Jesus when speaking to humans on earth states that you are God's and are part of your creator. See John 10:34–38 and 1 Corinthians 3:16, 17.

This is what the Bible is really saying when it states that humans are made in God's image and likeness, as Genesis 1:26–28 and Genesis 2:7 plainly states. When God said, "Let there be light," this was the beginning of the "third universe" and the beginning of the cosmos containing its billions of galaxies, planets, and moons together with all that was to follow, as God continued to create the physical universe and eventually intelligent humankind to enjoy another of God's unending creation.

THE CREATION OF THE HUMAN FAMILY

There is another far-reaching purpose for the human race that God has not spelled out in the bible which this book is going to give mankind a very brief glimpse into the future of God's plans for all those of the human race who undergo the final test of being perfected and tested as to their complete obedience to the rulership of Almighty God and their agreeing to all the rules of the eternal universe. See in the book of Hebrews 2:5–10 where it speaks of this very thing. In the book of the prophet Malachi 3:16–18, it speaks of a special book where those who serve God have their names written in it. Then see in the book of Revelation 20:11–15 as to what happens to all those whose names are not written in this book of life.

This subject will be discussed in much more detail later on in this book as to the future prospects of these ones who have their names written in the book of life.

THE GREAT REBELLION OF MAN AND THE ANGELS OF GOD

The creation of the physical universe, however, brought with it a division among the angels of God as we will discuss in more detail in this book and the problems that this has caused on planet earth. According to the book of Enoch, some two hundred of God's angels rebelled against the decrees of Almighty God regarding the physical world where each kind of the creation were designed to always reproduce their own kind. These rebels planned to go against this decree and proceeded to experiment with the DNA of individual species so as to produce hybrids and mixtures of the different kinds, such as some of the stories in ancient times of mermaids and unicorns, etc. The main reason for this rebellion is said to have been the desire of the angels to have sex with human women and to take wives for themselves, all whom they chose as Genesis 6:1–4 states. This will be explained in detail later in this book and what happened to these rebels as texts like Jude 6, 7 states.

ANGELS OF GOD MATERIALIZED AS MEN AND LUSTED AFTER HUMAN WOMEN

Imagine if you will, these angelic beings who the Bible states are far more powerful than humans materialized on earth as human men and then began to take human women as their wives who then began to produce hybrid creatures, known as the Nephilim, who were GIANT creatures who knew how to levitate things as their angelic fathers were around when the earth and mankind were created. We will explain in more detail later on in this book about how these creatures ruled in different parts all over the earth and about the many big monuments that they had created that are still in existence today, like Stonehenge, Easter Island, Pyramids, etc. (2 Peter 2:11) (Genesis 5:21-24)

HOW LONG WERE THE SIX DAYS OF CREATION?

In the remainder of this book, we will explain many of the mysteries that have mystified mankind for many millennia—things such as the large monuments in several different areas of the earth that have captivated the minds of researchers and scientists for centuries in their endeavors to try and explain them, such as the pyramids of Egypt as well as the giant statues of Stonehenge or the massive statues on Easter Island, just to name a few of the mysteries.

The second reason for these spirit beings as creators like GOD was for the purpose of creating intelligent physical creatures with the ability to recreate others like themselves perpetually so as to populate all the physical planets in GOD's ever-expanding physical universe. The planet earth is the testing place for perfecting individuals for that very purpose. (See 1 Corinthians 15:35–38. See also Job 38:7.)

Notice that all the days of creation mentioned in Genesis chapter 1 are all referred to in Genesis chapter 2 as "In THE DAY that GOD created both the heavens and the earth." (See Isaiah 55:8.) Isn't that interesting that GOD calls the whole six days of creation as THE DAY? Humans need to try and look at things from the creator's viewpoint that is beyond all the galaxies of this visible universe.

The Apostle Paul in Hebrews 4:1–11 refers to the 7seventh day of creation as still going on in his day, some four thousand years after GOD states in Genesis 2:1–3 that he has been resting from any more creation toward earth. Today, we are some two thousand more years into GOD's rest day, which is still going on and presumably will continue on through the one-thousand-year millennium of Jesus's rule. (See Revelation 20:1–6.) That means the days of creation are at least some seven thousand years long each, for a total of 7 x 7000 = 42,000 years and counting! God has purposely kept mankind from knowing exact ages of creation days.

GOD'S VIEW OF TIME

You will notice in the book of Genesis when referring to the days of creation that each day begins in darkness and ends in daylight. What does that mean? As an example, when GOD says, "Let there be light," and so over billions of earth years, a blink of an eye in GOD's time, stars begin to burst into life and begin to light up the previously dark universe. Finally after millions of more earth years, galaxies begin to form with all their millions of planets and star systems, including the earth, its sun, and the beginning of all that can be seen along with the invisible universe out of which everything else came!

WHAT IS TIME?

In order for humans to try and understand GOD and the physical universe, humans need to see things from a totally different point of view. For example, one must stop thinking as humans think in relation to time and space. See Ecclesiastes 8:17 as well as Isaiah 55:8, 9. One needs to ask, what is time? People on earth only know time by the time it takes for the earth to make one of its orbits around the sun, but this earth is just a tiny speck in this solar system that is another tiny speck in the Milky Way galaxy, which is another tiny speck in this vast universe made of billions of other galaxies!

GOD governs all three of the universes, both the visible and the invisible, as well as infinity, that other unfathomable universe. That other invisible "U" that involves about 95 percent of the known universe that is made up of dark matter and dark energy that scientists believe controls the visible universe by the effects that can be seen on the visible universe, much like the wind and gravity where one can see their effects on the physical world. Put yourself beside GOD outside of this physical world and imagine what you would be looking at with all the billions of galaxies swirling around you in a vast array of sparkling, brilliant lights and vast giant gas clouds in the process of creating more stars.

GOD'S ALLOWANCE OF TIME TO

CARRY OUT HIS PURPOSES

God utilizes time as humans view it so as to carry out his purposes. For example, he allowed time for the Egyptian nation to become a world power. In fact, it was the first world power of recorded history; and during that time, he allowed the people of Israel to become very numerous, so much so that the pharaoh became alarmed at the large number of them, being afraid that they might turn against the Egyptians and so decreed that all Israelite boy babies were to be killed. So the story of a deliverer became the only hope for the Israelites to escape the severe bondage that they now had to endure, after some four hundred years of their sojourn into Egypt.

This would become God's opportunity to show the world of that time his power over the Egyptians and to show the world who the real power is in this universe, of which the earth is but a small part. It was also an opportunity to show all the Israelites his power so that they might have more faith in the God of Abraham and his promise to make them a great, prosperous nation where all the other people of the earth could look to as a shining example of those who were blessed by the true Almighty God of the earth as long as they adhered to God's commandments. All these things that were allowed to happen took time, and God chooses the time that is best suited to carry out all his purposes, just as he has been allowing time for people of the earth to choose which path they will follow in their lives as they see what happens to those who follow the commands of God and to those who do not. This is just one of the allowances of time; another one has been for the purpose of choosing a special number of people from the earth who are to become kings and joint rulers with Jesus Christ during the one-thousand-year reign promised in the Bible.

This time, since Jesus was on earth, has been a time of testing for all these brothers-to-be of Jesus, as he was to be the first to be resurrected of many brothers who would become powerful spirit beings like Jesus as the Bible states in 1 Corinthians 15:44, 45; Hebrews 3:1; Hebrews 2:10, 12, 17, 18; and Revelation 5:9, 10.

GOD IS NOT GOVERNED BY TIME AS PEOPLE ON EARTH ARE

GOD is outside of and beyond the physical universe and is not governed by time as man regards time. There is no such thing as time, as earth people know it, in the realm of spirits where GOD governs the world by means of tens of millions of spirit beings that carry out his will (Daniel 7:9, 10).

As the universe is expanding, so does GOD, along with all mankind who have been expanding together with GOD. When one looks at things from GOD's viewpoint, it is easy to see that GOD's view of time is far different from man's ideas of time! Take the earth's star as an example. The sun takes about two hundred million years to make one orbit through the Milky Way galaxy at one hundred fifty miles per second.

THE DIFFERENT STAGES OF EARTH'S EVOLUTION

Today, science continues to evolve in its understanding of the physical universe where some have come to suspect that the earth itself may be older than the star it now orbits. They now have come to the conclusion that man has been on the earth for some millions of years and the planet itself probably some billions of years old.

The planet has gone through many stages in its evolution, including many of the stories about ancient people who were able to build and create the strange and gigantic structures such as the pyramids of Egypt and the giant stone circles of Stonehenge in England or the giant statues on Easter Island, among many others throughout the planet together with large population centers that have long since disappeared.

ONLY FOOLS IGNORE WHAT THEIR EYES SEE

For example, it would be very unwise to presume, as some pundits and so-called scientists have a tendency to do, that the creator of all the universes would not be able to manage to have a floating barge such as the ark that is mentioned in Genesis 6:14–16 where GOD could have preserved some eight persons together with a selection of specific animal species and be able to reproduce their offspring on the earth.

The size of the ark was to be about four hundred fifty feet long, seventy-five feet wide, and forty-five feet high and was to have three separate floors inside, giving it approximately about 1.5 million cubic feet of cargo space or about five hundred ninety railway stock cars of carrying capacity. It's interesting to note that modern ship builders have recognized that the dimensions of the ark were the ideal for stability, much as the super tankers of today. According to knowledgeable people, the ark would have been more than adequate to carry all the animals, food and people, birds, etc. Water would have been supplied by rain from the top of the ark, let down through a process of hollow bamboo poles to containers.

MANY LARGE VESSELS OF THE PAST WERE AS LARGE AS THE ARK

It's interesting to note that the further back one goes in history of past civilizations, the larger the shipping vessels were, such as the warships of both the Romans and the Greeks along with the Chinese vessels that plied the seas of old. Many were similar to the size of the ark. The ark, unlike those portrayed by Hollywood, was a plain rectangular barge designed to float, never to ply oceans. The majority of the animals were being the size of an adult sheep or smaller—and of course, they were all the very young that are the easiest to look after and would need the least food and would be the ideal ones to reproduce their particular species. GOD's angel shut the door.

THE OVERWHELMING EVIDENCE OF A WORLDWIDE FLOOD

There is much evidence throughout the entire planet Earth of such a worldwide flood having occurred in the earth's historic past that included some 277 flood stories from every part of the planet, with all kinds of physical evidence in places all over the planet such as mass beached whale skeletons in desert graves in the Sahara desert far from any sea. There have been many finds in Siberia of Giant Behemoths frozen with green tropical vegetation in their mouths and stomachs and dragonflies with two and a half feet wing spans in fossilized remains that have been discovered among many other signs of a sudden worldwide flood that covered the entire planet—and not just a local flood as some wrongly believe. See Genesis 7:19–24.

This flood changed the entire planet, including the atmosphere of the earth, which included a water canopy over the entire earth at the time before the flood that protected the earth from many of the harmful radiation rays from the sun and outer space, which also allowed the whole earth to be semitropical over all areas. This much heavier oxygen content in the atmosphere is the reason for the much longer life spans of people before the flood where people lived to almost one thousand years, such as Noah at 950 and Adam at 930, not to forget Methuselah at 969.

It's interesting to note that after the flood, the ages of people dropped dramatically, as Abraham, the friend of God, lived only one hundred seventy-five years, as ages continued to drop through the years following. The world now was going downhill further and further away from the perfect Adam and Eve. Just prior to our previous century, people were only living to about fifty or sixty if even that.

For more striking evidence of the flood, see *The Compelling Evidence of Noah's Flood* by Dr. Walt Brown of frozen birds, mammoths, and fishes found in sediment, with also trees that are aged at four thousand eight hundred years old. See also the many giant skeletons with BIG heads and double rows of teeth and six fingers on each hand and six toes on each foot on display in the Smithsonian.

THE OVERWHELMING EVIDENCE OF GIANT CREATURES BEFORE THE FLOOD

In the "Epic of Gilgamesh," it talks about an eight-foot-tall giant who is seen in a drawing holding a full-sized lion in his arms like a pet much like a normal human today holding a small house cat. This giant person called King Og is also mentioned in the Bible in the book of Deuteronomy 3:11 and refers to his bier as being about nine cubits long and four cubits wide by the cubit of a man. This also refers to the Rephaim who were from the Nephilim, the giants.

It is very interesting what the Bible says about this subject in the book of Genesis 6:1–4 where it states that there were GIANTS in the world in those days before the flood and also after that and tells about where these giants came from. They were a hybrid creation of the "sons of God," angels from the spirit realms who had entered the physical world of humans and took wives for themselves, all whom they chose and had sexual relations with these women so as to have offspring that became the mighty ones of old because of their giant sizes. Some were eight to twenty feet tall with six toes on each foot and six fingers on each hand with double rows of teeth. See 2 Samuel 21:20, Deuteronomy 3:11, and 1:28; 2:10, 20, 21.

The Bible explains a lot more about these creatures and why God had decided to destroy all of them along with mankind as well as the animals on earth that had been perverted from normal kinds that God had originally created. The earth was full of violence because of these hybrids who abused normal humans, forcing them into slavery to do their bidding and to build many of the giant monuments that are still seen around the world. They were also involved in experiments with mixing the DNA of humans and animals, thus creating the many weird creations of history, such as mermaids and unicorns, etc. The stories about these creatures are not fairy tales, as people have been told today, but actually were real creatures before the flood in past history of the earth. The giants knew how to levitate things like big blocks of stone such as the ones used in monuments like Stonehenge and others.

THE BIBLE EXPLAINS HOW THE BIG MONUMENTS WERE CREATED

The Bible is the only book that explains how it was possible for all of the giant structures that are seen all over the earth, some with absolute precision that are unexplainable even with modern machinery. These giant blocks in some cases weighed many tons that we today would still not be able to move. Some were one thousand tons and more. These giant creatures that the Bible says existed knew how to levitate things as well as their giant size were able to do many of the things that seem impossible to humans today. The other thing is that these angelic beings, the fathers of these giants, had a superior knowledge of creation as they had been involved in the creation of the universe as we can see in the Bible's book of Job 38:7, which sees them shouting out in applause at the Earth's creation, including the human race and all the animal creation.

According to the book of Enoch, it states that some two hundred of God's heavenly angels left their proper place in the spiritual realm and materialized physical bodies so as to be able to have sexual relations with human women as the Bible stated in Genesis 6:1–4. The Bible tells us what happened to these angels that did this and to just what God ordained regarding them in the book of Jude 6, 1 Peter 3:19, 20, and 2 Peter 2:4, 5. They are in a type of prison.

These two hundred are not the ones that are continuing to try and corrupt mankind today. These are the other rebels that followed Satan in his rebellion. The book of Job gives us an insight into what goes on behind the scenes where it shows Satan continuing to try and turn people away from God. It is very enlightening to see how the Devil continues to taunt God about each person on earth. Try reading the account for yourself if you have ever wondered why bad things happen to good people in Job chapters 1 and 2. These are the ones referred to in Revelation 12:4, 7, 8, 10, and 12. They are referred to as one-thirds of the angels that followed Satan in rebelling.

THE REASON FOR A WORLDWIDE FLOOD

All the reasons were already discussed. The giant offspring had spread out all over the planet, and it is the reason why God had to bring a worldwide flood in order to destroy all of them together with everything that they had created, including all the hybrid creatures and their offspring that were bullies just like them and that were ruining the earth and God's original plans for the earth to be a paradise, just like the Garden of Eden in the beginning.

The worldwide flood was the most humane way to get rid of all these evil ones, along with all their offspring and what they had been attempting to do in trying to change the everlasting covenants of God that they had been experimenting with the DNA of different animals and mixing it with human DNA so as to create other types of species, against God's law of kinds that only reproduce the same kinds. Things such as mermaids, unicorns, etc., were not just fairy tales, as some believed.

This was the reason for God having Noah build a giant-sized ark so as to preserve alive all the different species of animals that God had created in the beginning, along with Noah and his small family together with all the food that would be needed. And God would have his angels gather together all the animals at the appointed time and bring them to the ark, which was just a floating barge not meant to ply the oceans but merely to float. And of course, all the animals would be the very young, the easiest to look after and the best ones to reproduce afterward.

Water would have been supplied from the roof of the ark by the rain during the flood and let down to water all the animals, birds, as well as Noah and his family. Unlike Hollywood movies that always portray big elephants and other adult animals, only the very young would have been gathered to go into the ark. The ark would have been quite capable of holding all the about twenty-one thousand species that God wanted preserved. It had a capacity of about five hundred ninety rail cars and able to carry some one hundred eighty thousand animals the size of an adult sheep, and most are smaller than that.

THESE DIMENSIONS OF THE ARK ARE THE PERFECT SIZE

These measurements of the ark are said to be the most ideal dimensions for stability and are similar to the modern supertankers. It's very interesting to note that the further one goes back in history, the larger the vessels are that we find, such as the Roman and Greek warships, together with the Chinese and trading ships of the past. Also, the further back we go, the larger and more complex we find the structures—maybe the reason for all these complex creations were because these people back there were closer to the perfection of Adam.

And to think—as most evolutionists do—that the Creator, the Supreme God, would not be able to have an ark constructed to preserve all his creation through the flood should take a good long look at their own marvelous human body, not to mention the complex human brain that allows them to reason on the very things that they see, with the very special eyes that allow them to see in vibrant colors the marvelous creations all around them. They should be ashamed of themselves as to how ungrateful they are to give the credit to the blind creation rather than to the creator of all this wonderful world that God made for man to enjoy and to experience this treasure chest, the planet Earth.

The Bible in Romans 1:21–25 rightly refers to them as both EMPTY-HEADED and very foolish to deny what their eyes see all around them and above them. The Bible states in Isaiah 40:26 to raise your eyes high up and see who created all this wonder. We didn't do it, did we? Someone must have, as we know that there is not a thing that is created that does not have someone that created it. The house that you live in or that car or truck that you drive did not create itself, did it? So our common sense cries out to us that someone must be responsible for the millions of galaxies and billions of stars and millions of planets and moons—all must have had a creator.

A WORLDWIDE FLOOD OF GIGANTIC PROPORTIONS

In order to cleanse the earth and to destroy all the creations of the giant hybrid creatures in many different parts of the earth, it was necessary for GOD to bring this deluge that would change the entire earth and cleanse the planet of all these giant creations, along with the giant offspring of these hybrid creatures. This was the only merciful way to cleanse the entire earth. See these texts at 2 Peter 2:4, 5; 3:5, 6; and Jude 6 as to what happened to their angelic fathers who were put in prison and were preached to by Jesus as recorded at 1 Peter 3:18–20 after his resurrection from the dead.

The Bible suggests that humans are more than flesh in many passages, such as Genesis 6:3 where it states that man is more than flesh. It is also spirit as in Ecclesiastes 12:7 where it shows that the flesh returns to the earth, but the spirit returns to the spirit realms where GOD is. So when these hybrids were destroyed, their fleshly parts went back to dust, but their spirit part was left to roam the earth as demons such as the ones that Jesus ordered out of some poor individuals as recorded at Matthew 8:28–32 and Luke 8:28–32; 10:17–20.

MANY DEMON SPIRITS STILL ROAM THE EARTH

There are also many demon spirits still roaming the earth as there were in the time when Jesus was on the earth, such as the ones mentioned in the texts above and also in Mark 9:20 that indicated a deaf and dumb spirit, along with the case where Mary Magdalene was possessed with some seven demons that were ordered out of her by Jesus as shown in Luke 8:2.

In the book of Job 1:6 and 2:5, it shows that Satan, the Devil, is still seen as going back and forth between heaven and earth and causing many problems for individuals on earth whenever and wherever this demon can, as it is allowed to do by GOD. Please read the experience that Job had with the Devil. It is very enlightening to know what is happening in the world and why!

THE REASONS FOR THE COMPLETE DESTRUCTION OF ANCIENT PEOPLES

Who were these people of certain nations and/or tribes that God had commanded the Israelites to completely destroy from the face of the earth from all males and to include both women and their children? How could a God of love command the Israelites to do such a horrendous thing? What possible reason could require such drastic action against a whole race of people who were inhabiting these lands that God was going to give to the nation of Israel as their possession to time indefinite?

Let us look at the history of these people that were to be destroyed completely and see if this command was in fact justified. What type of people were they, and what did they practice as a nation? Some of the things that we will discover as we look at their history is their practice of child sacrifices where they would sacrifice their children to their false gods to appease them as well as burning some of these poor little ones alive. Does any of this sound familiar as to what is happening in the area under the control of the group known as ISIL in the modern Middle East?

These people also practiced the magical arts, inquiring of the dead, dream tellers, etc. These practices were all condemned by the Supreme God of Israel, and anyone found practicing any of these things were to be put to death so as to prevent these evil things from being like a cancer that would eventually lead people away from the true God of Israel who had just delivered them from bondage in Egypt.

These godless practices of these pagan people were to be avoided at all costs by the entire nation of God's chosen people who were to be an example to the rest of mankind as to what happens to people who worship the one and only true God of the whole earth and how they were to be blessed of all the people on earth. The purpose of God was to prove that he alone is the one that controls all things, including the weather, the rains for their crops at the right times the sunshine, and the blessings of healthy families and who were to become a great and feared nation by all the other nations of the earth. This was the reason for the complete destruction of all those people that practiced the evil things.

WHO WERE THESE PEOPLE THAT WERE TO BE DESTROYED, AND WHAT WAS THEIR ANCESTRY?

Here is a list of the nations and their tribes that were to be eliminated from the earth by the command of the Almighty God, the Creator of all things!

	These were the sons of the An-a-Kim,
AMORITES	Deuteronomy 1:28; 2:10, 11; 12:31
HITTITES	
AMALEKITES	All these people were from the Nephilim!
JEBUSITES	See Genesis 6:4 and 11.
CANAANITES	They were from the sons of the Anak who were all "GIANT-SIZED PEOPLE" that could be traced back to the people before the Flood that God destroyed!
PERIZZITES	
AIKING	

When we take a close look at the evil practices of these people, we can start to see just why God had them destroyed. An example is in Deuteronomy 12:31 and 13:1, 5, 10, 11; 18:11, 12. These texts show the reasons for God's decision to have all of them destroyed, as we can see also in the book of Joshua chapters 10 through 13. These include the infamous Philistines and all the Geshurites who were all from those same evil people before the Flood!

The Bible connects the Nephilim to the Rephaim who were sons of the Anak (Numbers 13:31–33 and Deuteronomy 1:27, 28; 2:10, 11, 20, 21, 34; 3:6, 7; and 7:2–6, 25). As we examine the situation that Israel faced, we can start to see just why these evil nations deserved to be destroyed completely from the earth. Today, we are seeing the very same thing happening in the Middle East with the evil ISIL group.

GIANT CREATURES STILL ON THE EARTH AFTER THE FLOOD

There are many places in the Bible that refer to giant creatures still on the earth in the times after the Flood, such as the giant that David, the future King of Israel, slew as recorded in 1 Samuel 17:4, 49 as well as in Numbers 13:32 and 33. In the book of Revelation 18:2, it states that a symbolic woman, who is referred to as a prostitute because of its mixing religion with the politics of the world, is a place of dwelling for demons. The suggestion is religious because it is a place where marriages take place, as Revelation 18:23 shows, and includes all of Satan's false religions of the world!

And in Revelation 12:3, 4 and 12, it shows Satan, along with its demon followers, being cast out of heaven and down to the earth; and "woe to the earth"; for Satan is going about the earth like a roaring lion seeking to devour anyone it can because Satan knows that it's time for ruling, and ruining the earth is about to end in the very near future. Soon now, GOD's kingdom is about to come!

WHAT IS THE SPIRIT IN MAN?

The Bible, in many passages, shows that there is a difference between the person of dust and the spirit that dwells within the person, such as the example given when Jesus ordered the demon spirits out of people as recorded at Matthew 8:28–32. And note the difference between the soul or the spirit and the body of flesh at Matthew 10:28. In the book of Psalms 146:4, it shows that the spirit goes out, and the body goes back to the dust of earth. When Jesus died on the stake, his last words were: "Receive MY SPIRIT," and Stephen said the same at his death. See the following texts in Luke 23:46 and Acts 7:59, as well as in 1 Corinthian 2:11, 12 and Ecclesiastes 12:7 that shows the difference.

WHAT IS THE SOUL IN ALL HUMAN BEINGS?

The Bible shows that the human soul includes three parts—the same as their creator—namely, SPIRIT, MIND, and BODY. One SOUL and GOD, SON, and SPIRIT equals one GOD. That is how man is made in "the image of GOD," not the same in body but made of the same stuff or essence, for GOD is all and everything!

The Bible again, in Hebrews 4:12, shows that there is a difference between soul and spirit. Here, the Apostle Paul shows that the Word of GOD is sharper than a two-edged sword and is able to the dividing of soul and spirit.

WHO OR WHAT IS THE "WORD OF GOD?"

The Bible, in John 1:1, 14, states that the "Word of GOD" became a person of flesh and blood and was with GOD in the beginning and was itself GOD, not "a god" as some translations try to imply. This one was to be called Jesus and is referred to as the EXACT IMAGE of the INVISIBLE GOD (Hebrew 1:3 and 1 Timothy 6:16). There are so many texts that show that Jesus, while in the flesh, was a perfect image of the father and made the claim that he and the Father were one and the same, such as in John 10:30. In John 14:8, 9, Jesus says that he is GOD, the Father. In John 17:5, Jesus shows that he existed before the world was ever created and shared GOD's GLORY.

In John 17:17, Jesus states that GOD's word is "the Truth." In John 14:6, Jesus claims that "he is the truth." In 2 Peter 3:5–7, the Bible states that the worlds are held in place by the Word of GOD. In Hebrew 1:1–3, the Bible shows that all the systems were put in order by GOD's Word; and in the book of Colossians 1:15–18, again, it shows that the Word is the IMAGE OF GOD!

THE WORD AND GOD ARE ONE AND THE SAME

In the Bible book of Isaiah at 55:11, it shows that the Word of GOD will not return to GOD without results that were ordained by GOD; again showing that when GOD speaks a word, it must come to pass, as GOD is ALMIGHTY! Again, in Isaiah 45:22, 23, it shows that GOD and HIS WORD are one and the same, and there is no one else like GOD! In Isaiah 46:9, 10, GOD again states that there are no other like God but he himself as THE SUPREME GOD! Compare Romans 11:34–36 and Hebrews 2:10 as well as Colossians 1:16 that refers to Jesus.

WHO IS THE "FIRST AND THE LAST?"

The Bible, in Isaiah 48:12, 13, GOD claims to be "the First and the Last"; and with his own hands, he created all things. In Isaiah 44:24, Yahweh states that he alone created everything; and in Isaiah 44:6, GOD again states that he is "the first and the last" and that there are no other gods like the SUPREME!

Isaiah 43:10–12 states that there are no other gods but Yahweh. There never was and there never will be! At Isaiah 42:8, it states that GOD will not share his glory with anyone else; and in John 16:15, it shows that all of GOD's glory belongs to Jesus! In Isaiah 9:6, where it is a reference to Jesus, it states that he is to be called MIGHTY GOD, PRINCE OF PEACE, ETERNAL FATHER. See also Matthew 23:9.

In John 8:58, Jesus claims to be the "I AM." In Exodus 3:12–15, the ALMIGHTY GOD states that he is the "I AM" when speaking to Moses. In Revelation 1:8, 13–18, and 2:8, this shows in no uncertain ways that Jesus is "the First and the Last" just as Almighty GOD claims to be as in the book of Isaiah 44:6 and also in Revelation 22:13 and 16 where Jesus is the A and Z!

JESUS WAS RAISED AS A LIFE-GIVING SPIRIT

Jesus resurrected his physical body or one like it for the purpose of showing it to Doubting Thomas as proof to the rest of his apostles as well that he was alive from the dead. It's interesting to note that in the several times that he appeared to the apostles, they did not recognize his physical appearance but rather his voice or mannerisms. For example, when Mary met him at the tomb, she thought that he was the gardener and asked him what they had done with the body of Jesus (John 20:14–17).

Only after Jesus spoke and said Mary did Mary believe that it was the Lord Jesus, but Jesus said, "Do not touch me, as I have not yet gone to the father." No doubt because he was a spirit at that moment and not a flesh and blood body as 1 Corinthians 15:44, 45 states that Jesus was raised up as a spirit, a life-giving spirit.

SPIRITS DO NOT HAVE PHYSICAL BODIES

Jesus, now as a LIFE-GIVING SPIRIT, has all authority over heaven and earth; and because spirits do not have physical bodies, Jesus was now able to walk through locked doors and appear in the room where the apostles were assembled, as in John 20:19 and 26 and Luke 24:36–39. Jesus now has the power to appear in whatever form he chooses, just as certain angels in the past have been able to do, such as when they appeared to Abraham and then to Lot in Sodom to warn of the coming destruction. See Genesis 18:2–9 and 19:1, 5, 11–13.

People need to realize that in order for Jesus to pay the ransom price for all mankind, it meant that he would have to forfeit his physical body and would no longer have a physical body rather now, a powerful spirit being like GOD!

WHO GOES TO HEAVEN AND WHEN?

The question has always been who of mankind ever go to heaven? This is an age-old question that deserves a Bible-based answer. The first? One needs to ask: what was GOD's original purpose for mankind? For example, if Adam had not disobeyed GOD, would he not still be here on earth? Sin is the only cause of death. Does that not answer the age-old question? Man was never meant to go to heaven, as the book of Psalms states that "the meek shall inherit the earth," so why does the Bible say that some people are destined to eventually go to heaven? We need to find out who these ones are and why do they go to heaven and not the rest of mankind (Psalm 37:11 and 29)? GOD's promise is to make the earth into a paradise. See Isaiah 65:17–25.

The promise of GOD in the Bible is for the earth to one day be made into a paradise, where people and the animals will all be at peace with one another, and people will live in peace with one another with no more wars. There will be no more of animals killing and eating other animals either, with the wolf and the lamb feeding together as one! So where did the idea come from that most religions believe and teach that they are all going to heaven or hell?

GOD'S PROMISE: A PARADISE EARTH

According to the Bible, heaven is the realm of GOD and angelic beings or spirits. It was never GOD's purpose for humans to become spirit beings. In Revelation 5:9 and 10, it states that Jesus has bought people for GOD from out of all nations of earth with the purpose of making them into spiritual KINGS who are to rule with Christ Jesus for a thousand years. (See Revelation 20:4–6.) The next question is this: who are they to rule over? The Bible answers in the book of Psalms 37:9, 29. The next question is how many humans are taken from earth. The Bible answers at Revelation 14:1–3. (They are limited to one hundred forty-four thousand.)

WHAT IS THE KINGDOM OF HEAVEN?

According to the Bible, the kingdom of heaven is made up of spirit beings, that is why Jesus, when he was asked about it, said that the kingdom of GOD is in your midst in Luke 17:21. Jesus's first disciples were some of the one hundred forty-four thousand who would eventually make up the heavenly kingdom that is to rule over the earthly part of GOD's kingdom. See Revelation 6:9–11, 1 Thessalonians 4:13–17, and 1 Corinthians 15:50–53. See Luke 12:32 where Jesus refers to the kingdom and promises his "little flock" that they were to inherit that very kingdom!

THE NEW HEAVENS

When the Bible refers to the promise of GOD to create a new heaven and new earth, what does that mean and entail? In Isaiah 65:17 where this promise is made, it shows what the new earth will be like, but we need to go to the book of Revelation 21:1–4 that shows what the new heavens will accomplish for the new earthly part of GOD's kingdom. In Revelation 20:4–6, it shows that these are the rulers, the new Jerusalem that is seen coming down from heaven, the bride of Christ, his one hundred forty-four thousand associate kings in Revelation 21:2, 3. This is the heavenly kingdom that will rule over the new earth that would have been cleansed of corrupt earthly governments and would have been replaced by people picked by Christ Jesus.

THE NEW EARTH

This is really the answer to the Lord's Prayer at Matthew 6:10 where Jesus was telling people what they should pray for: "Let thy kingdom come, let thy will be done on earth as it is in heaven." The new earth referred here is not a new planet but rather a righteous new government guided by the heavenly kings and Christ Jesus, which is to replace the many corrupt nations and kingdoms of the world today that are presently ruining the earth. See GOD's warnings in Revelation 11:18; 2 Peter 3:3–13; and Psalms 2:2–12.

GOD'S ORIGINAL PURPOSE FOR PLANET EARTH

The original and final purpose of Almighty GOD is to see that his original plan for the planet Earth is to be carried out to the letter, including that planet Earth is to be a literal paradise with all human beings living on it in perpetual unity, happily serving each other and acknowledging Almighty GOD as their loving benefactor, Yahweh or Jehovah GOD. See Isaiah 66:22

EXPLANATION OF THE MYSTERIES

Let us sum up the entire picture of GOD the Creator, the universe, and the earth and man upon the earth in this way to explain the many questions everyone has about how certain things are possible—things that Jesus was able to do when he was here on earth. Curing sickness and/or disease, raising people back to life from death, walking on the water or levitating on it, and commanding the wind are just some of the several miracles Jesus did. Let us begin to answer these mysteries and many others that have mystified mankind for ages.

In today's world, many modern scientists believe that the earth, the universe, and mankind have all evolved from the instant in time that is referred to as THE BIG BANG to what we see and are today! This includes the billions of galaxies, composed of tens of billions of individual star systems including the earth and it's sun and associated planets, moons, and including how mankind has evolved from primitive humans to the very intelligent beings of today who are concerned about the condition of the planet and are attempting to try and correct global warming that has been causing major disasters in all parts of the planet, as well as discovering many strange, unexplained aspects of the past history of the planet. Many of these mysteries will be explained later.

REASONING ON THE

STATEMENTS OF JESUS

Now, let us reason on some of the things that Jesus stated and showed when he was on earth. Just some of the things that he was able to control were the energy atoms of this physical universe by the fact that he was able to cure the many different illnesses and diseases instantly, even bringing a person back from the dead (John 11:43, 44 and Matthew 12:15). He told his followers that they could do the same things and even greater things than these if they would only believe and have faith. What was Jesus really saying when he stated these different things about the possibilities of people being able to do miracles?

FAITH CAN MOVE MOUNTAINS

Look at the situation when Jesus was found walking over the stormy sea and where Peter asked him if he could come to him over the sea, where Jesus told him to come and Peter was able to walk on the water until he became afraid because of the windstorm and started to sink and cried out to Jesus, "Lord, save me!" Jesus then held out his hand to rescue him and said, "Why did you doubt?" You see, Peter was actually walking over the water before he began to doubt that he could do what he was, in fact, actually doing! What does all this suggest to us? Please read the statement by Jesus in Matthew 14:25–33.

GOD CONTROLS INVISIBLE ENERGY

So just to go further into this subject, mankind needs to recognize that all matter is just a form of energy coalesced, and the vibration of atoms slowed to become a visible mass. Invisible atoms of energy are what the creator has in abundance, some 95 percent of the known universe. This energy exists, and like the wind, scientists can see its effects on the physical universe, and that is a fact. GOD controls all of it like the grand puppeteer that the Bible claims it to be! Why do so many of mankind find it so hard to believe in these realities? We know that the universe exists; that is a reality we all agree, and according to the Bible, that real being that created it all is GOD through his all-powerful Word.

WHAT IS THIS MIND OVER MATTER?

Finally, an explanation of what exactly is the all-powerful WORD of GOD. This Supreme Being is the one that controls the entire cosmos, both the invisible and the visible one. Just how does this being create things? You have all heard of "mind over matter." Well, notice Jesus's words about this subject in the Bible in Matthew 8:26, 27 where Jesus commands the wind. Notice what happens instantly—it quits blowing, and the sea is told to quiet down. According to the witnesses who saw what happened, notice what they said in verse 27: "Who really is this person, where even the wind and the sea obey him?" In Matthew 14:25–32, Jesus is seen walking on water by levitating in thin air, again showing his control over physical matter. In this incident, Peter was able to do it too until he began to doubt himself.

FAITH CAN MOVE MOUNTAINS

In Matthew 17:20, Jesus further states, "If you had as much faith as a small mustard seed . . ." which is one of the smallest seeds, you would be able to command a mountain to be removed and cast into the sea, and it would do exactly what it was told to do. That is kind of hard to believe, isn't it? Especially when you have been programmed all your life to believe that you CAN'T do things like that, you can't do this or that. That is why it will take about one thousand years to reprogram mankind's brain to be able to realize their full GOD-given potential as those who are made in the image of their creator!

In Matthew 21:19–22, Jesus commands a fig tree to wither up and die, and it did. Jesus again states that if they had just a little faith, they could tell the Mount of Olives to be moved over into the sea, and it would obey you! On one of several occasions when some, just by touching Jesus garment, were healed, Jesus said to them, "Your faith has made you well!" See Mark 5:25–34, again, showing that mankind has the same abilities that Jesus had if they had faith!

WHAT IS GOD TELLING MANKIND?

It's interesting to see how the Bible explains this very thing where it shows that certain spirit beings, the angels, rebelled against GOD's way of doing things and entered the physical world as physical beings and took human wives for themselves, all whom they chose and had sex with them, whereby they were able to create hybrid offsprings that the Bible refers to as the Nephilim who were GIANT creatures among normal humans. See Genesis 6:1–4.

These GIANT hybrid creatures had amazing powers, such as being able to levitate things, which there angelic fathers obviously knew how to do and which these hybrids and their angelic fathers used to lord it over normal humans. This was the reason why GOD decided to destroy all that evil world that was against the everlasting covenants of GOD where these beings had been experimenting with the DNA of animals and humans and had been teaching humans how to create weapons to kill things with, and so the earth was full of violence and immorality, much the same as it has become today. And we know what happened last time, so this should be a serious warning for the world today, shouldn't it? See Genesis 6:6, 7 and 2 Peter 3:3–7, 10–12, and you will now know how GOD feels about what happens on this planet!

HOW THE UNIVERSE WAS CREATED

This is how the present worlds were created by this all-powerful being that is able to create out of the ethers of the universe by the power of an-all powerful mind everything that now exists, both the invisible and visible world. This is what Jesus showed in a small way by the things that he was able to do by curing all people's diseases or blindness, hearing, etc., as well as the control over the wind and the sea. And because mankind is a physical image of that Supreme Being, they also possess these same powers, if only they could believe and have the faith that Jesus showed by the things that he did.

THE REPROGRAMMING OF MANKIND IN THE MILLENNIUM

From the time that one is born into this physical world, one is taught to believe what their parents have taught them as truth, such as "You can't do this" and "You can't do that," so we can see why it is so difficult to believe Jesus when he tells us the opposite things, such as if we but look to GOD and have faith, there are all kinds of things that we CAN DO! UNFORTUNATELY, it is a very difficult thing to do in order to undo that which all mankind have been taught to believe for some thousands of years.

It will take a thousand years of earth time to reprogram the human brain to change to the thinking of Jesus and to be able to do similar things like what he did. The millennium of Christ, the one thousand years of his future reign over this planet is what this will accomplish, mainly to bring the human family back to perfection, what GOD intended in the beginning of the creation of the physical world.

Then man will start to finally realize his full potential as a being that truly represents the image of his invisible creator with abilities beyond his wildest dreams and imagination, just as Jesus promised. If you would only have faith and believe, nothing will be impossible for you. See 1 Corinthians 2:9–15.

LEVITATION WILL BE WONDERFUL

I know and believe that even now, mankind should be able to levitate, not just things but oneself, as I have done many times during sleep. I can tell you, that is a wonderful feeling of power; that is mind over matter. It is something that will be a natural ability when mankind is finally brought back to perfection. Just imagine one will never be afraid of falling off a cliff or drowning as one will be able to just walk over the water just as Jesus was able to do and to never having to fear anyone or anything anywhere on the earth anymore. This is the promise of our loving GOD and Creator of all that is! BELIEVE IT!

MANKIND'S AMAZING FUTURE AS CHILDREN OF AN ALL-POWERFUL GOD

In many instances, Jesus showed that mankind would be able to do unimaginable things in the future, much the same as Jesus did. It makes a lot of sense, since man is made in the image of GOD, the Creator of everything in this wild and wonderful universe of which man is a vital part, with the same creative abilities as the great GOD who made man in his own Image. Man has an indomitable spirit, but the fleshly part is weak as Jesus said when he was faced with the cruel death that his fleshly body had to be subjected to (Matthew 26:38–41).

The final conclusion of the matter is this: We are all faced with things that are happening in today's world that fit many of the signs that Jesus said to watch for just before his return to the earth to set up GOD's KINGDOM over the earth. Note some of these signs that mankind was to watch for:

- FIERCE STORMS ALL OVER THE PLANET
- MAJOR AND MINOR EARTHQUAKES
- DEVASTATING FLOODS IN MANY AREAS
- NUMEROUS WARS ALL OVER THE WORLD
- PLAGUES SUCH AS THOSE IN AFRICA (EBOLA)
- TERRORISM SUCH AS THE ISIL KILLERS
- GLOBAL WARMING AND ITS CONSEQUENCES
- ANGUISH OF NATIONS WITH NO ANSWERS
- REFUGEES FLEEING FOR THEIR LIVES
- IMMORALITY WITH NO NATURAL AFFECTION

> *Please read 2 Peter 3:3-13 and 2 Timothy 3:1-7.*

Jesus stated that those who see these things happen before their very eyes will see the coming of the KINGDOM of GOD! See Matthew 24:3–39 and Luke 21:25–36 where "the meek shall inherit the earth" (Psalms 37:29).

NO ONE KNOWS THE DAY OR THE HOUR

As the Bible states in Matthew 24:36, no one knows the exact day or hour of Jesus's second coming, and the reason for this is because GOD knows the human heart and how treacherous it can be. For this very reason, GOD intends to allow humans the opportunity to prove themselves either lovers of righteousness or lovers of evil, such as the ISIL group in the Middle East. GOD allows this so that they may be judged according to their works, whatever that may be, so one needs to be aware and ready as Matt. 24:44 states, so the choice is ours to make, as GOD has given each generation that choice.

EVERLASTING CUTTING OFF

The Bible shows that the Devil's future is one of eternal cutting off from life, as it has disobeyed the everlasting covenant of the universe that decrees everlasting cutting off from existence and applies to all those who choose to follow in the Devil's footsteps. Each person must make their own choices in this life as free moral agents that GOD has decreed as the search continues for suitable people to populate the planets in an ever-expanding universe!

GOD'S MEANS OF SALVATION

See Matthew 25:41, 46 and ask: where do I stand on this most important? Are you for a righteous new world or the old one that is ruining the earth? See GOD's warning to those who are ruining this beautiful earth in Revelation 11:18. Are you willing to conform your life to the righteous principles of GOD's laws and able to accept GOD's means of salvation through the ransom sacrifice of the perfect life of Jesus Christ that he provided for the sins of all mankind? The choice is for each person to make and to show their acceptance by the way they live their lives in the time remaining where GOD has shown much patience in order that as many as possible are able to make the right choice. Please read 2 Peter 3:3–13; 2 Timothy 3:1–7 and 12–17; and Matthew 25:31–46.

THE NEED TO KNOW THE TRUTH IN ORDER TO PROTECT YOURSELF FROM THE WILES OF THE DEVIL

Everyone needs to examine their standing in relation to the requirements as stated in the Bible for all those who will inherit everlasting life in GOD's kingdom. Note what is said about this in the Bible in John 17:3 about the need to "the taking in knowledge about God and Jesus Christ." This does not suggest leaving it up to someone else, like a minister, rabbi, priest, or any other religious group.

The reason that it is necessary for each individual to take in a personal knowledge about God is because every person must answer for themselves to God, so you cannot leave it up to anyone else. And if you are to do this successfully, you need to know what you need to do personally to achieve to eternal life. See Matthew 7:7–23 to read what Jesus said about this subject.

We need to look at more of these requirements. In Mark 10:17–22, it shows the many difficulties of some individuals in their quest for everlasting life. Notice what things that really defile a person in Mark 7:14–23 as Jesus explains these to the crowd. In Matthew 22:36–40, Jesus again states the real requirements for all those who would gain God's approval. In Ephesians 6:10–17, Paul shows how one can protect oneself from the machinations of the evil enemy of all people—that is, Satan, the Devil, who is looking to turn people away from God and their sure hope of salvation through faith in Jesus Christ, the Lamb of GOD.

This evil creature according to the Bible is going about in the earth like a roaring lion seeking to devour everyone it can in order to turn people away from the truth by trickery, deceit, and outright lies, pretending to be an angel of enlightenment. See 2 Corinthians 4:3, 4 and 11:14, 15. Also 1 Peter 5:8–10 and Matthew 16:27.

FAITH APART FROM WORKS IS DEAD

The Bible in 1 Peter 2:2:21 shows what all those who would gain salvation must do by looking to Christ Jesus as your perfect example to follow, one needs to look at Jesus and ask oneself as to what would Jesus do in any given situation that one may be faced with in life? See James 2:16–26.

Did Jesus, for example, acknowledge the need to bow down to anyone? Especially false gods and those whose desire is to be like the Supreme GOD, as was the case of Satan, the Devil, when it attempted to get Jesus to bow down to it? Matthew 4:8–10 says the promise to give Jesus "all the kingdoms of the world" if he would just BOW DOWN to the devil.

What was Jesus's answer? "Go away, Satan, for it is written, you must worship the true GOD only and not bow down to anyone." The Supreme GOD never asks anyone to BOW DOWN! Is that not interesting? How, unlike these false gods and all those rulers and monarchs of this world who demand such allegiance of their subjects, most are insecure, egomaniacs, and tyrants? True deity does not have any needs!

The people who are bowing down to these false gods are only worshipping a lesser god, as one who desires to be like the one Supreme God. Sadly, these have been deceived into bowing to the false gods of this old world, and the Bible shows this to be the case, as Satan continually pretends to be, as the Bible calls it "the god of this world" who is shown to be a liar and murderer as in John 8:44, 45. See John 12:31 and Revelation 12:9 and 12.

As another example, many of these religious Christian leaders have taught their followers that it is okay to be involved in the politics of the world, of which Satan is the god and invisible ruler of this system of things, that is ruining the earth (Revelation 11:18). Can you imagine Jesus voting for any of the rulers of this old world?

WHAT IS THE FRUITAGE OF YOUR RELIGION?

The main thing to watch for in any religion is to look at the kind of fruitage that it produces in its followers. For an example, see what is happening in the Middle East. Among these followers of the Koran religion, this group, ISIL, are bent on killing and beheading and raping poor women who have been brutally treated as well as like slaves, completely opposite to the teachings of Jesus where his followers are told to "LOVE one another" and "Do to others as you want others to do to you."

THOSE DECEIVED BY SATAN

The behavior of this ISIL group is the same as the god that they profess to worship and show their allegiance to by falling down to this sadistic monster, about five times a day, to the false god of this old world that is alienated from the true GOD! How sad for all these poor people who have been deceived by Satan. How different are the teachings of Jesus. For example, in Matthew 5:44, Jesus's followers are encouraged to "LOVE their enemies and to even PRAY for them." Isn't that a beautiful statement?

Now let us consider religions that profess Christianity but do not follow the teachings of Jesus, for example, the taking part in the wars of Satan's world, the so-called Christians killing other so-called Christians, dropping bombs on people leaving millions dead. This is totally opposite to the teachings of Jesus GOD's law of "Thou shalt not kill." Read what Jesus says about these religions in Matthew 7:21–23.

Still, there is another reason for individuals to be very careful about leaving salvation in the hands of others or any religion that is not producing the fruitage or following Jesus's teachings. By this, you will know them, by the LOVE that they do or do not show to each other and to the rest of the world. See Matthew 5:44–48.

WHAT IS THE FRUITAGE OF THE WORLD'S RELIGIONS?

You will know them by the fruitage that they produce in many of their followers. As an example, do they encourage their followers to take part and be involved in the politics of the world, of which the Bible states that Satan is the ruler? (John 12:31 and Revelation 12:9 and 12.)

Many individuals of the churches of the different persuasions in Christianity do not follow the teachings of Jesus, and the reason for this is because they have not been told of the truth by the clergy of their religion. Instead, they have been deceived into believing it is okay to be a part of this old world, which is in total opposition to the teachings of the Bible. As an example, many religions are now agreeing with same genders being married in the church and that homosexuality is not that bad, even though it is totally contrary to the teachings of the Bible and Jesus Christ. See how the Bible views these things in Romans 1:26–28 and 32; and 1 Timothy 3:2 and 12.

THE HYPOCRISY OF RELIGIONS

Many of the religions are even agreeing with so-called scientists who believe and teach that modern mankind has evolved from apes or chimpanzees. Isn't it interesting that these same creatures that presumably were the progenitors of mankind are still all here with us today? As far as one can tell, they still look the same as they always have, although the Bible states that those who believe and teach such things are EMPTY-HEADED FOOLS who give credit to the creation for everything instead of to the CREATOR, the Almighty GOD (Romans 1:20–25). Many of these religions go on and continue agreeing with these evolutionist theories of creation.

EMPTY-HEADED EVOLUTIONISTS

Would any semi-intelligent person think that things such as cars, trains, planes, houses, and everything else created themselves? The answer is obviously no, and yet many so-called scientists and all those who entertain the same beliefs would have us think and believe that the far more complex universe and the human brain and the fantastic human body itself—which is a miraculous functioning energy machine—all were created by blind evolution! How utterly foolish to entertain such empty-headed thinking, just as the Bible states in Romans 1:21, 22 and Isaiah 40:22, 23, and 26.

THE FALSE DOCTRINES OF MANY OF THE WORLD'S RELIGIONS

There are so many false teachings by so-called Christian churches, along with other faiths, that are totally contrary to the belief of the GOD of LOVE, such as the belief that this GOD of LOVE has created a special place in order to torture certain individuals, not for just a while but endlessly and for all eternity. How unbelievable this must seem to any intelligent-thinking person, and what a contradiction to the belief in a GOD of LOVE! Yet so many, if not most, of the world's religions believe and teach this sadistic idea to their followers. What a contradiction this must be to any normal person.

ANOTHER MONSTROUS LIE OF SATAN

Any normal-thinking person can hardly believe that the God of love who has stated in the Bible book of Genesis 1:31 that everything that God has created is seen to be "very good" cannot possibly now suggest that such an evil idea ever existed in the mind of this God of Love, nor could any sane person ever attribute such an idea to this GOD of LOVE that the Bible shows God to be! Obviously, this is just another monstrous lie of Satan, the opposer of truth, who is constantly trying to turn people away from the true GOD by perpetrating such evil LIES and then blaming God for them, with the idea to make out that God is a sadistic type of god.

This is why those humankind who know the truth from the Bible and, by their use of common sense, have the responsibility of exposing these lies about our loving creator to everyone that will listen to reason and truth because of all the harm these lies have done to so many people and continue to do in turning still others away from GOD and the belief and faith in Jesus Christ.

THE FATHER OF ALL LIES

In order for the true followers of Jesus to carry on this war against these lies of the devil, one needs to be able to prove where they began and by whom. In the book of Genesis 3:4, it states that an invisible voice pretending to be a serpent told Eve the first lie—that she would not die if she disobeyed God, where God had told Adam that they would die and go back to dust, as Genesis 3:19 says. Notice what Jesus said about this in the book of John 8:44, 45.

DOES THE HUMAN SOUL CONTINUE AFTER DEATH?

I believe that we can all agree with what God said—that mankind does die and goes back to dust—so here was the first lie. If we look in the Bible in Revelation 12:9, we see that the Bible calls this evil one. Satan is referred to as the original serpent, the same one that lied to Eve in the Garden of Eden, pretending that a serpent was doing the talking. There was another instance in the Bible where another individual heard a voice from a voiceless beast of burden, as quoted in 2 Peter 2:15, 16. Satan, who is an invisible spirit, continues to deceive mankind by using physical creatures such as the serpent that it used to deceive Eve to continue to fool mankind.

LIES ARE EXPOSED BY THE TRUTH

That is why the Bible refers to him as the great deceiver. Satan had to create another lie to back up his first lie by saying that people do not really die, but some parts of the body goes to either heaven or hell after death. See Ezekiel 18:4, 20 and Ecclesiastes 9:5, 10 as to what the Bible says about this subject.

So the question we need to ask ourselves is this: Does my religion teach these things? And if they do, should I continue to support a religion if these beliefs are what is being believed and taught? The answer should be obvious. The next question then must be: what should I do about my relationship with God and Jesus Christ? The answer is found in the following texts of your Bible in John 17:17 and 18 and John 17:3. You need to ask: why the religions of this world do not teach the truths found in the Bible? Might they be the very ones spoken of in 2 Thessalonians 2:9–12 as those who have been misled by the devil into believing his lies and teaching them to their followers? And like many others throughout history, have they allowed themselves to become corrupted by the great deceiver, Satan, who the Bible shows is misleading the entire world that he controls? And until God brings this wicked system of things to an end, by setting up his own kingdom under Christ Jesus, all those who are looking forward to the coming of that kingdom on earth must do what we can to show—by our works in relation to our faith —that we really believe in the promises of God in Isaiah 65:17–25 and Revelation 21:1–4.

WHAT HAPPENS WHEN THE HUMAN BODY DIES?

According to the Bible, they simply cease to exist—no thoughts or any awareness of anything—simply as asleep but no dreaming (Ezekiel 18:4, 20; Ecclesiastes 9:5, 10; and Romans 6:23). They do not go to HEAVEN, as so many religions teach, but rather to the common grave condition where they stay asleep until the last day when the general resurrection is to take place that is known as the great white throne judgment (Revelation 20:11–15). This is a time far into the future after the one-thousand-year reign of Jesus Christ where the earth by now would have been returned to a paradise condition (John 11:11–14).

Read what the Lord Jesus says about this in the book of John 12:48 where it is referred to as the last day. See John 6:39, 40, 44, and 54. So the question one needs to ask is: when does this take place that is mentioned in Revelation 20 above? The Bible shows the sequence of events that is to take place before the one-thousand-year reign of Jesus.

In the books of Matthew and Luke, Jesus is asked by his disciples as to when would this present system of things be brought to an end. And Jesus then gives an entire list of things that they need to watch for that would indicate the generation that would see the coming of God's kingdom rule over the earth. See Matthew 24:1–44; Luke 21:10–31; 2 Timothy 3:1-5; 2 Peter 3:3–12; Daniel 12:2–4; and Malachi 3:16–18.

According to the Bible, no other humans have gone to heaven other than Jesus and the one hundred forty-four thousand until judgment day, which is not until after Jesus's one-thousand-year reign over the earth (Revelation 20:4–6).

It is of utmost importance to have a correct understanding of all these things, as the Bible shows that there are two resurrections as shown above. The first one applies to only the future kings, the one hundred forty-four thousand humans. These have been bought from the earth and include the twelve apostles of the Lamb. These are to rule over the new earth and all those people who have the hope of living forever on a paradise earth (Psalms 37:29). Notice too that the second resurrection does not take place until after the first resurrection and the one-thousand-year reign of Jesus over the new earth. It is then that the thief who died beside Jesus will be resurrected, as Jesus promised in Luke 23:43, along with all of the rest of mankind (Revelation 20:11–13).

IS THE BIBLE STILL RELEVANT TODAY?

According to the Bible in Revelation 12:9, the Devil is misleading all the entire inhabited earth, so would that not include all the world's false religions who have prostituted themselves by being a part of this old world that is an enemy of the true GOD? See 1 John 2:15–17 and John 17:14, as well as Romans 10:2–4. It would have to include all those who are a part of Satan's old world that is ruining the planet Earth. It's important to remember that there may be many LIES, but ONLY ONE TRUTH, and that source is the everlasting reliable WORD of GOD in the HOLY BIBLE!

THE INFALLIBLE WORD OF GOD

The Holy Bible, GOD's infallible Word of Truth, has been preserved throughout the centuries in spite of many attempts to try and destroy its relevance and never more so in today's world that is now once again under Satan's final onslaught because he knows that his time for ruining mankind and the earth is about to end. So Satan is attempting to make people believe that they have outgrown the moral truths and ideas in the Bible, with the modern twisted thinking of today's world that is spiraling out of control where the politicians of the world under Satan's influence have no answers to the breakdown of human society in many nations.

This is the real danger of people believing Satan's lies—that all the ideas and beliefs in the Bible are outdated and that the now modern world's ideas of rape, murder, and immoral acts are now not that bad and that doing your own thing in any and all the many situations of life is acceptable to modern society and is all okay now. But look at the disastrous results of broken homes, divorce, and just living together without any legal documents that has caused such suffering to so many families and the world in general.

There is no peace and certainly no security in today's world, and most of all, there is a lack of real love for one another and very little for people of one's enemies. How different this is from what the Bible states about the real Christian faith. See 1 Peter 4:3–9; John 13:34, 35; and Matthew 5:43–48. This is the real danger of a civilized society collapsing when God's laws are ignored.

TRUE BELIEVERS MUST LIVE THEIR FAITH

All those who would live a true faith must keep themselves apart and separate from the world—that is, drifting away from the truth in God's word into mankind's theories of evolution that has been designed specifically by Satan to create atheists and unbelievers and to create doubts even in true believers of God, with the intension of turning them away from God into its teachings of immorality! See these texts in James 4:4, 7 and 1 Peter 4:4, 5; and 5:8.

The one true faith must be in harmony with all the teachings and beliefs in God's Word and cannot be a partaker in the politics and wars of this old world, of which Satan is the invisible ruler and god of this system of things (1 John 5:19 and John 12:31 and 16:11). A true believer and follower of the Lord Jesus must show they are doing that by the way they live their lives as an example to all, as true Christians, and not to carry on as the world does that is now alienated from the teachings of God in the Bible (James 2:19–26).

THE NEED TO DEMONSTRATE FAITH BY SHARING THE GOOD NEWS

The true faith does not necessarily have to be in any particular place or belong to some man-made organization, but individuals need to show by example and by deeds of godly devotion by their speaking to others about their faith and sharing the Good News at every opportunity with others. See Romans 10:11–15, 1 John 2:1–3 and 15, and 1 John 5:3 and 11, 12. By this, they show love of GOD!

The good news about God's way of salvation through the faith in Jesus Christ is what the whole world needs to hear; this is the obligation of every individual Christian and should not be left to any church or religious organization. It is such "good news" that each Christian must share it with everyone that will listen because of their love of other human beings. See Matthew 28:19, 20. When one looks at the dangerous conditions of early Christians in their endeavors to sharing the "good news" in the Roman times and where they were in danger every day of losing their lives, we today have no such problems, and yet how many Christians even bother to talk to others about the "good news" today? Where is that love?

HOW TO RECOGNIZE THE TRUE CHRISTIAN RELIGION

How can one recognize the true Christian faith looking at what the Bible states in 1 John 5:19? That the true faith must not be a part of the world of which Satan is the god and where their followers are busy at every opportunity, telling others the "good news" about the KINGDOM of GOD and their faith in Jesus Christ. See Matthew 24:14.

If you know of a religious organization that fits the description stated above, by all means, join with them and continue telling others about GOD's way of salvation through the ransom sacrifice of Jesus Christ, the only Begotten SON of GOD. One hears much about the word, truth in the world, and many wonder what is TRUTH. When Jesus was asked that question, here is his answer: "My Fathers Word is the truth! And in another text, Jesus states that "I am THE TRUTH AND THE LIFE! No one comes to the Father except through me" (John 14:6). As the living WORD of GOD, Jesus is GOD, just as John 1:1 states along with many other texts.

For example, in the first part of the Bible, in the book of Isaiah 44:6, GOD claims to be "the First and the Last" and that there is no other GOD but the Supreme GOD Yahweh (Isaiah 45:5). And to no one else will God give or share his glory, as Isaiah 42:8 states, and then in Isaiah 10:21 where it is referring to GOD. It refers to GOD as MIGHTY GOD and then in Isaiah 9:6 where it is referring to Jesus. It states the same thing to him, calling Jesus the MIGHTY GOD, Eternal Father, Prince of Peace, again, showing that YAHWEH and JESUS are one and the same.

There are many other texts in the Bible that show that Jesus and GOD are one and the same in the spirit world, where Jesus originated from as the eternal Word of God, as John 1:1 and 14 states. Also, Jesus was to be known as IMMANUEL, when translated, means, GOD with US in the flesh and blood of JESUS!

We will go into texts in more detail in the New Testament portion of the Bible to show how they agree with the ones in Isaiah that we have just discussed that show that Jesus was and is the all-powerful, Almighty, INVISIBLE GOD, Creator of all that is" (Matthew 1:23).

THE TRUTH ABOUT WHO JESUS REALLY WAS ON EARTH

There are many example texts in the Bible where GOD claims to be the First and the Last, and the Beginning and the End, the Alpha and Omega. Note what the book of Revelation says in Revelation 1:4 and 8 where it is referring to the Almighty God, Yahweh, as the Alpha and Omega. In verse 17,, he claims to be the same and says, "I am the First and the Last." And notice the description in verse 14 about Jesus and then compare the description of the Almighty God in the book of Daniel 7:9, 10, and 13 that shows again "someone like the Son of Man," just as the book of Revelation 1:13, 14 that states about this one, Jesus.

Then note in Revelation 22:13 and 16 where it again is referring to Jesus and makes the claim that he is the Alpha and Omega, the First and the Last, the Beginning and the End. Last, in Revelation 1:18, it is made completely clear that Jesus is the one that "became dead" but is now living forever and ever and has the keys of death and Hades, which is a symbol of the common grave of all mankind.

There are many other texts in the Bible that compare Jesus with GOD, such as Colossians 1:15–18 that shows Jesus, as the Word of God, had created all things. Then compare this with Hebrews 1:1–3 that again shows that Jesus is the exact PHYSICAL image of the INVISIBLE GOD and is referred to as GOD in verses 8 and 10 who created all things including the heavens, the spirit world, and the physical universe, including the earth and mankind. Compare Isaiah 55:11 and 44:24 and then examine Isaiah 42:8 that refers to God's glory and that God will not share "glory" and

John 17:5, 22; 16:15 that shows GOD's GLORY is JESUS GLORY. See also Philippians 2:11.

THE TRUTH ABOUT HELL AND OTHER FALSE BELIEFS

Let us now consider some of the false teachings and beliefs of the many different religions of this world that Satan has deceived into teaching some of his lies, such as hell, where individual souls are to be tortured and tormented forever with no chance of parole. Many world religions believe and teach this monstrous lie of Satan.

WHERE DID THIS PLACE CALLED HELL COME FROM?

The question we need to ask is: where did this place of "hell" come from? This idea of a place where poor unfortunate souls could go, to be endlessly tormented and tortured? And who created it? It must be someone other than the GOD of LOVE because such an idea could not possibly have come from the God of love, as such an idea would be the complete opposite of love. So who is responsible for this horrible idea?

In the book of Genesis 1:31, it states that God has just pronounced that all the creation that God has made is VERY GOOD! One can now hardly believe that the God of love who has just stated the above—about all the things that have been created—could not possibly include such a horrible place as hell, that all these false religions would have you believe.

This idea must have come from the great enemy of God and truth, namely from the same one that told the first lie in the Garden of Eden, Satan the Devil. In order to cover up its first Lie, it has to create still another lie, where it attempts to get people to believe that just the physical body dies; but something that is invisible, such as an immortal soul, lives on that no one can prove or disprove how convenient, and the exact opposite of what God states in the Bible in Ezekiel 18:4, 20 and Ecclesiastes 9:5, 10.

RELIGIONS WHO TEACH THIS MAKE GOD OUT TO BE A SADIST

What a contradiction this idea of a place of torment must be to any normal-thinking human being who believes in the God of love! One must ask this question of these religious leaders who believe and teach this monstrous lie of Satan: why do they suggest and make God look like a sadist, much worse than any of the evil dictators of human history?

Still, another question we need to ask is this: Is it the purpose of a loving God in just keeping some poor soul alive so that it can be tortured forever? Does that make any sense? Why not just get rid of them? Why keep them hanging around? And just imagine, if it were really true, and one or some of these poor souls were related to you, such as your mother or father, how could you possibly now enjoy living in paradise knowing that they were in this place being tortured night and day forever and ever?

SATAN'S LIES DO NOT STAND UP TO THE TRUTH

When one breaks down these lies of Satan, we find that they do not stand up to true scrutiny or to any commonsense thinking. For example, what purpose would God have to seek some kind of revenge or punishment for whatever it is that they had done in life? With regard to his perfect justice, how would torturing someone for all eternity, for whatever they had done in one lifetime here on earth, be equal to forever in God's perfect justice? I do not believe that any of even imperfect mankind's justice would say that such a decree was justice and would, in fact, be far away from any sort of perfect justice! One can see how ridiculous this idea of Satan is when confronted with reason and common sense. See John 8:44.

The answer to all of these questions is: why have religions created all these lies about God, hell, and an immortal soul? Might the reason be so that they might exercise complete control over their followers by the use of fear, which is the exact opposite of what GOD is—LOVE! We need to remember that there are only two emotions that govern all of mankind—LOVE and FEAR. GOD represents LOVE, and Satan uses FEAR to control mankind; and the choice is up to each person as to whether they choose to live their lives in fear or choose GOD's way of LOVE! Please read what the Bible states in the following: John 14:23–27; 15:7–10; and 17.

THE REAL MEANING OF HELL AND HADES

The real meaning of the word *hell*, as it is used in the Bible, is far from the idea that religions have told everyone, so let us look now at its real meaning. Both the words *hell* and *Hades* have the same basic meaning of a cold, dark place, which is the common grave of all mankind where Jesus also went to at his death (Acts 2:31, 32).

It was from hell that Jesus was resurrected. Revelation 20:13 says that hell and Hades is the common grave where all the dead are. In the book of Daniel 12:2, this is also made very clear. In the book of Psalms 16:10—that is referring to Jesus—it states that God will not leave Jesus in Sheol or hell, again showing that hell and the grave are one and the same condition or place.

WHAT HAPPENS TO HELL INDICATES WHAT IT REALLY IS

In the book of Revelation 20:13, the Bible shows exactly what hell and Hades represent, as it shows the sea giving up those who were DEAD in them. Notice that all are DEAD in both of these places and not in some place where they had been conscious and having been tortured, as false religions would have you believe.

What this is really showing is that both hell and Hades mean the common grave of mankind. Notice also that death is thrown into Gehenna as well. So because death is done away with, there is no reason for hell or Hades anymore because there were no more graves.

The next thing we need to know about is: just what is Gehenna? It is stated to be the lake of fire. We need to understand that this language must be a symbolic language because of who and what is thrown into it. Why do we say that? The reason is this: look at what is thrown into it—DEATH, which is a condition and not real substance, and hell or the common grave, again a place that is all over the earth and even in the sea.

In Revelation 20:10, it shows the wild beast and the false prophet are both thrown into this place, along with the Devil in the final judgment. If this were literal language that were being used here, we would have to ask: just who is this wild beast? Is it a lion or maybe an elephant or a wolf? Any person who is open to reason can see that this lake of fire really does symbolize everlasting cutting off from life, just what Jesus shows in Matthew 25:41 and 46. Please read it for yourself.

ALL THOSE NOT IN "THE BOOK OF LIFE"

We need to take special notice of the timing of when all these different things are hurled into Gehenna. The Devil, together with the wild beast, the False Prophet, and all those who do not have their names written in the book of life. Notice that all things, people, and the symbolic beast and false prophet, together with Death and Hades or hell, are all going to be done away with, just as Revelation 21:4 and 8 states in plain language where this shows that this symbolic place, the lake of fire means THE SECOND DEATH. Just as the dead were not conscious in the common grave, nor are those here either. They simply will cease to exist anymore.

THE NEW HEAVENS AND THE NEW EARTH

The next thing we see in sequence in Revelation 21;1–4 after the end of all evil and wickedness on earth and including death itself is the picture of a new heaven and a new earth, along with the Holy City, New Jerusalem, coming down out of heaven. Notice that there are two heavens mentioned here. So let's first explain these two heavens.

This new heaven is likened to a bride adorned for her husband. Who is this bride? And what does she symbolize? The Bible shows us that this bride really means the one hundred forty-four thousand ones who have been purchased from the earth, as in Revelation 5:9, 10; 14:1; and 20:4–6, and John 3:28–30 where John shows that Jesus is likened to the bridegroom and his future disciples that would become his symbolic bride as Revelation 21:2, 9, 10, 14, and 24.

The old heavens that are no more and which represented the old system of things under the invisible rulership of Satan, the Devil, which included all the present systems of things of mankind that had been ruining the earth. This is what the new heavens is seen to be replacing. This invisible old heavens of Satan and his demon followers are the ones seen being cast out of heaven in the book of Revelation 12:9. These same ones are to be cast into Gehenna at the final judgment, as at Revelation 19:19, 20 and 20:10 includes Satan.

WHAT IS THE NEW EARTH?

The new earth is a cleansed earth and not a new planet as so many wrongly believe, as this beautiful planet was designed by God to last forever, as in Isaiah 45:18. God does not have to go to all the trouble of creating a whole new planet, that is why the Bible in Revelation 11:18 shows God stating that "he must bring to ruin, those ruining the earth." The new earth is referring to all those who are seen as the ones that are spoken of in Isaiah 65:17–25 and includes all the meek who are to inherit the new earth, as Psalms 37:29 states, and includes all described in Malachi 3;16 and would include all those people who have put their faith in the hope of everlasting life in a paradise earth that Jesus said would include all those putting faith in his ransom sacrifice as stated in John 3:36; 5:24–29; 6:51–54 and 58.

THERE ARE TWO ERAS OF THE NEW HEAVENS AND EARTH

There are two separate eras of these new places, so let us explain the first one about the new earth that is spoken of in Isaiah 65:17–25. This time period that is referred to is the millennium of Jesus Christ where the earth is in the process of being restored to a paradise condition. See 1 Corinthians 15:24–28.

Notice too that some of the conditions that are shown to exist in the new earth, such as the animal kingdom where all the animals are at peace with one another as in Isaiah 65:25. Note what is said in relation to humankind where a boy of one hundred years of age is considered as a youth, as people will live much longer lives in the new earth, as old as trees, which is NOT FOREVER! That is one of the main differences that is shown in Revelation 21:3, 4 as to the time or length of life, which is indicated to be forever. Still, another big difference is that this passage says that GOD himself will be with mankind, and he will wipe away all the past sorrows, including the main one; and DEATH will be no more, another major difference.

THE ROAD BACK TO PERFECTION

It is during the millennium of Christ that people will be given the opportunity to reach to mental and physical perfection, as Adam was in the beginning where he lived nearly one thousand years, at the ripe old age of nine hundred thirty, and then died. It is during the millennium of Christ that the reprogramming of the human brain in all the people will be one of the main educational programs carried on so that they might reach their full potential as children of Almighty God.

These will have many of the abilities that Jesus showed when he was on earth as a perfect human soul, such as the ability to be able to levitate things as well as themselves, together with many of the miraculous things that Jesus showed that it will be possible for all humans to do when they finally gain to perfection. Look at some of these words of Jesus in Matthew 14:25–33; 15:30; and 31, Matthew 21:19–22, Mark 11:20–24, Luke 8:23–25, and Luke 17:6. One of the main things one can see from these texts is the importance of showing that you have faith in GOD!

THE DIFFERENCE OF THE TWO HEAVENS

The new invisible government of Jesus Christ, that is referred to as the new heavens, is comprised of Jesus along with his one hundred forty-four thousand associate kings who are to rule over the whole earth for the one-thousand-year millennium of Christ's kingdom, where their responsibility is to return the earth to a paradise condition, along with the entire human population. It is to replace the old heavens, along with the Devil and his demon followers together with all the many corrupt governments who have been ruining the earth under the control of Satan for the past some six thousand years of recorded history.

These evil rulers under the invisible rule of Satan have been the ones responsible for all the evil things that have happened on the earth, along with the establishing of separate nations and the cities and their resulting pollution and the many problems that go along with them such as crime, high taxes on the people in order to support them, and the real danger to all people living within them, such as dangerous earthquakes that take place all over this living planet with the danger of people by the thousands being killed in these high-rise apartments and other large buildings or apartments, as has already happened in many places. And look at the wars and the horrifying aftermath of destruction all over the earth. Is there any doubt about who is really ruling the earth? See Ephesians 6:11, 12.

GOD CONFUSED THE LANGUAGES

One can start to understand why God confused the languages of early humans and to stop them from starting to build a city that was to be called Babel because it was there that God confused the languages so that they could not understand each other and so were forced to give up in their endeavors to build cities. See Genesis 11:1–9. We can now see the wisdom of God because God could foresee the dangers of building cities, such as stated above.

Please read the following texts: 2 Corinthians 4:3, 4; 11:14, 15; and 1 Corinthians 10:20. We today are continually being warned and told that major cities are going to experience major earthquakes in their areas, and it is just a matter of time before a major catastrophe will happen. When one looks at these high-rise buildings with thousands of people in them, there is sure to be hundreds of casualties and injuries.

THERE ARE TWO DIFFERENT RESURRECTIONS THAT TAKE PLACE

Who are involved, and when do these two resurrections take place? These are the questions. Let us examine the first resurrection and just exactly who are these "special ones" as the Bible indicates that they are. Jesus gives us the first clue as to who these ones are in the books of Matthew 22:30–32 and Luke 20:34–36 that state that those who are worthy of that resurrection are as the angels, neither can they die anymore. Then we compare this with the book of Revelation 20:6 that confirms that this is the first resurrection.

So these people who take part in the first resurrection are now as the angels or spirit beings just like Jesus when he was brought to life as a life-giving spirit as 1 Corinthians 15:44 and 45 indicates. The last one, that is the last Adam referring to Jesus as the last perfect one created by God, is now able to grant everlasting life to others.

THE LITTLE FLOCK'S NAMES HAVE BEEN WRITTEN IN HEAVEN

The book of Luke contains more evidence that shows just exactly who these ones are in Luke 10:17–20 where Jesus indicates to his intimate apostles and followers. Their names have been enrolled in the heavens and are to be a part of the "little flock," who are to inherit the heavenly part of the kingdom of God. See the text in Luke 12:32–34. That is why Jesus could say to them that the kingdom of God is in your midst because they were to be the ones that would make up that heavenly part of the kingdom.

Jesus shows that there are two separate flocks in his followers, as in the book of John 10:16 where he says that some are not of this fold of the "little flock" who have the heavenly hope of eternal life as spirit beings like Jesus. These others are to become part of an earthly kingdom of God as Psalms 37:11 and 29 says about the meek who shall inherit the earth!

And finally, in the book of Revelation 20:6, it shows these ones who take part in the first resurrection are those who make up the one hundred forty-four thousand associate kings that Jesus refers to in Luke 20:36 who are to rule over the earthly part of the kingdom of God in order to make it into a PARADISE EARTH.

WHAT HAPPENS AT THE FIRST RESURRECTION?

It is at this time in the history of the physical universe that all the one hundred forty-four thousand chosen and counted worthy ones who are either being brought back from the dead in the first resurrection or the rapture of the remaining ones who are still alive on earth at the presence of the Lord in his second coming. See 1 Thessalonians 4:15–17 and Revelation 20:6.

Next, we see the Devil and his followers are cast into the abyss and have it shut over them so that they are not able to mislead the human race anymore until the one-thousand-year reign of Jesus is over. After which, they must be let out for a little while. See Revelation 20:1–3.

Next, in the book of Revelation 21:1–4, we see the new heavens, the Holy City, the New Jerusalem coming down out of heaven from God prepared as a bride adorned for her husband. Notice that this is not just some individual woman but rather an entire city—NEW JERUSALEM—and just as the old earthly city of Jerusalem was the capital city of Israel, so this is the capital city of the heavenly Jerusalem that is a spiritual city coming down from God.

This city is made up of the one hundred forty-four thousand chosen ones of God who have been bought from the earth to rule as kings over the new earth. See Revelation 14:1–3 and Revelation 20:6 under the leadership of Jesus Christ.

THE NEW HEAVENS REPLACE THE OLD HEAVENS

This is the new spiritual invisible government that is now to replace the old invisible heavens of Satan, the Devil, who have been ruining the earth and misleading the nations of the world and causing untold suffering to mankind by evil wars. See Revelation 12:9.

We notice in Revelation 21:1–3 that the "tent of god" is with mankind, as a protector to all the earth, and shows how it will end all the past sufferings that are to be no more, including death in verse 4. We can read in more detail these conditions that are to prevail on the new earth in Isaiah 65:17–25 where it shows that the animals and mankind will all be at peace with one another.

WHAT IS THE SECOND RESURRECTION?

According to Revelation 20:5, the rest of the dead of mankind do not come back to life until the one-thousand-year reign of Christ is ended. We see Satan being released from his prison in the abyss as soon as the one thousand years are over. Satan is going out to try and mislead all the nations in the four corners of the earth to gather them to the war, to see how many of them that he can get to join him in this final rebellion against God, much the same no doubt by trickery, as he did in the Garden of Eden with Adam and Eve.

Now as all people on earth are in a state of similar perfection by the end of the one thousand years, there is an entire population of perfected people who are to be tested as to their choices. Are they going to allow themselves to be misled by Satan so as to rebel against God and join Satan in his final rebellion? These are to be numberless as the sand of the sea, and all these rebels advanced over the earth to wage war against God's people, but fire came down out of heaven and devoured them. The Devil, who was misleading them, was thrown into the lake of fire. This is the final end of Satan where the wild beast and the false prophet already are, as Revelation 19:20 states. This is the second death.

THE SECOND RESURRECTION AND THE FINAL JUDGMENT

Next begins the great white throne judgment in Revelation 20:11 that signifies the second resurrection of all the dead in Hades, hell, and the sea who all give up those dead in them. And the scrolls are opened, including the scroll of life, and all the ones whose names are not in the scroll are cast into the lake of fire, which means the second death that symbolizes being cut off from life for ever and ever—in other words, destroyed eternally.

It is only then that we see the fulfillment of the promises of God come to fruition, where all the tested and perfected people of the new earth will now see the earth as "the perfect paradise" that God had ordained it to become in the Garden of Eden! See these texts in Revelation 22:1–5 and 21:1–4 and Matthew 25:34, 40.

WHAT IS THE LAST DAY THAT JESUS REFERS TO REGARDING THE RESURRECTION OF THE DEAD?

In order to answer this question that Jesus refers to in a number of places in the Bible such as John 6:40–44 where he promises his followers that he will resurrect them at the last day, we need to determine when exactly this day takes place. The first text we need to examine is found in Revelation 20:5 that states that the dead do not come to life until after the one-thousand-year reign of Christ Jesus, which is far into the future. The next question is: when does the one thousand years begin and end? How can we know when the first resurrection is to take place? See Revelation 12:7–10.

The Bible tells us that it takes place after the war of Armageddon where Jesus and his angels win the war in heaven and throw the devil along with his demon angels out of heaven and down to the earth. Woe to the earth because the devil knows that the end of his rule over the earth is near at hand and so is going about in the earth like a roaring lion seeking to devour anyone and everyone that he can.

The things happening on the earth in the world today would suggest that we are seeing this happen, as the signs that Jesus said to watch for are all happening before our very eyes. Jesus said that those who see these things will also see the end of the present wicked system of things that is ruining the earth that the Devil has been responsible for, including all the terrible things that are happening today. You can read about these signs that Jesus said would happen just before the end of this system in Matthew 24:3 to 44 and Luke 21:7–31. These signs are what to watch for regarding the coming of the kingdom of God and the first resurrection.

This "last day" is known as the great white throne judgment where all the dead that are in the memorial tombs are to come back to life and to face the judgment, as in John 5:25–29 where Jesus is speaking of that very thing to all his followers. So the last day follows the final end of Satan and all those who follow him in their final rebellion as recorded in Revelation 20:7–10. It is right after this takes place where all the dead in the memorial tombs are resurrected to life or eternal death in what the Bible calls the second death, the lake of fire! This is the second resurrection where all mankind are finally judged (Revelation 21:8).

PLANET EARTH: "MAN'S TREASURE CHEST" A GIFT FROM GOD

This beautiful planet is a real treasure chest filled with everything that makes life interesting and enjoyable from an abundance of a variety of foods to satisfy everyone's desires and appetites. Plus, all kinds of precious things, such as gold, silver, diamonds, and an endless supply of precious gems have made the earth such a real treasure chest for mankind to enjoy from a loving creator.

Doesn't it remind you of Easter egg hunts when you were young and how enjoyable it was to search for those Easter eggs? This whole planet is like that with an abundance of hidden treasures waiting to be discovered. How wise God is to have made such a beautiful home for his children, so diversified and so interesting that people are never bored. That is not an easy task; only God could have achieved such a miraculous home for all mankind.

Just think about what a marvelous creation this is and the speed that the earth is travelling at as it swirls through the galaxy in its orbit around the sun at some sixty-six thousand miles an hour, plus spinning on its own axis at another one thousand miles per hour at the equator and 105 miles per second as the sun drags it along with it in its orbit through the galaxy. And just think about that; it has been doing this for thousands of years, travelling at these fantastic speeds through all kinds of debris other planets and their moons, and it hasn't run into anything yet.

Isn't that fantastic? And all the so-called brilliant scientists and evolutionists would like us to believe that there is no one piloting this rocket ship we are on. There is no one in charge of it all.

I like what the Bible says about these people who give all the credit to blind creation rather than to the creator, where it calls them EMPTY-HEADED in Romans 1:21–25. Just think of that; we on this beautiful planet are travelling at about four hundred forty-five thousand miles per hour, and you don't even know it, nor are we all falling off, thanks to another miracle called gravity! Then there are all the interesting seasons that we all can enjoy, where the weather is always changing, that makes life interesting.

MANKIND ARE ALSO SPIRIT

The Bible in many of its texts shows that mankind are more than flesh and blood but are also spirit beings like their father who is the great spirit, Almighty GOD. That is why the Bible states that mankind are made in the image of God. When we look at what the Bible says about God in John 4:24, it states that GOD is a "spirit," and all those worshipping God must worship God in spirit and in truth! So if God is a spirit, and we are made in his image, would that not suggest that we are also spirits? That would seem to make perfect sense!

In the book of Genesis 6:3, this seems to be saying exactly that, where it states that man is also flesh, which would infer that he is also spirit, wouldn't it? And if we turn to another book in the Bible at Zechariah 12:1, this says that God formed the spirit of man inside the person of flesh. In Ecclesiastes 12:7, this shows that when the body dies, it goes back to dust, but the spirit goes to God in the realm of spirits. This again shows that there are two separate parts to the human person that separate at death.

And again, still in another text at Ecclesiastes 3:21, it says that no one really know whether the spirit of mankind goes up or whether it goes down, again stating that man is part spirit! Notice what Jesus says about this very thing at John 6:63 that says it is the spirit that is life-giving, whereas the fleshly body is of no value at all. When we look at the following texts in the Bible in 1 Peter 3:18, it says that while Jesus's body of flesh perished, his spirit was resurrected as a life-giving spirit as recorded in 1Corinthians 15:45 and is referred to as the second Adam.

Still another text that is very interesting is in 1 Peter 4:6 that states that the good news was preached to the dead in regard to their fleshly bodies but that their spirit lives should live according to the spirit. And in Ecclesiastes 11:5, it intimates when the spirit is about to enter the baby in the womb of a pregnant woman in order to create another human soul that is made of flesh and spirit! This harmonizes with Genesis 6:3.

MANKIND ARE SPIRITS CLOTHED IN FLESHLY BODIES WHILE HERE ON EARTH

So in looking at all of the evidence from the Bible texts, one must come to one conclusion—that man who was made in the image of his father who is "pure, invisible spirit" is also spirit in a body of flesh, just as Jesus was while here on earth. We are not comparing ordinary mankind with the special son of God because Jesus was not born in the flesh to an imperfect father as the rest of man have been. That is why the Bible in 1 Corinthians 15:45 speaks of Jesus as the second Adam, as he was to be born perfect in order to buy back mankind from sin and death.

Many people—because they are not aware of who they really are—cannot understand why bad things happen to very nice people in this present world where the Bible states that the Devil is the main cause of all the terrible things that happen to people! The Bible says that Satan is continuing to taunt God about all the people where Satan continues to try to get them to deny God and to do things against what God has asked people to do in practicing love for one another and to even love enemies.

Think of this planet and your life here as a testing ground for God's spirit children who are being put through all sorts of trials in order to perfect them for their lives in God's creation. That is why in the Bible in 1 Peter 1:14–16, it states that all of God's children must be made holy because God is holy. This is the real purpose while you are here on earth. These tests are all toward that end. See the reason for this in Hebrews 12:5–11.

There is an interesting text about this in 1 Corinthians 15:38 where it is talking about people being resurrected and where it states that God gives them a body as it pleases God in keeping with his law of whatever a person sows. They must also reap, so this tells us that one should be very careful what they have sown.

WHAT IS GOD'S KINGDOM?

The question that we need to address is: what is a kingdom? What is involved? What is the territory? Who are the rulers? Who are the subjects?

Let us look at these questions one by one. Jesus talked about this kingdom in what is known as the Lord's Prayer in the book of Matthew 6:9 and 10 where he told his followers to pray for God's kingdom to come, and his will to be done on earth as it is in Heaven. So the territory is the whole planet earth. Next, who are the rulers of this new kingdom that encompasses the whole planet? The Bible answers this in the book of Revelation 20:4 and 6 that tells us that this is Jesus and one hundred forty-four thousand associate kings who have been bought from the earth, as in Revelation 14:1–4 and 5:9, 10.

This new kingdom of God is referred to as the new heavens that are to rule over the new earth as recorded in the book of Isaiah 65:17–25 that talks about the conditions that life will be like in that new earth.

So the next thing we need to discover is who exactly are the subjects of this new earth? If we look at texts in the book of Psalms 37:11 and 29, this tells us who these ones are, where it says that they are the meek and teachable ones who have put faith in God's promise of the coming kingdom of GOD to be ruled over by Jesus, their Savior and King.

The new rulers of the new earth are said to have been bought from among mankind and have washed their robes in the blood of the Lamb, which means that God has accepted them as his spiritual sons by their following in the footsteps of their Savior and have proved themselves faithful by their work of bearing witness to the good news about God's kingdom and Jesus Christ as their Lord and Savior. This is the work of all Christians to bear witness to Jesus! See Acts 1:8 and Matthew 28:19, 20 where Jesus states this very command to "go and make other disciples, teaching them to observe all the things I have told you!"

The purpose of the kingdom is to make over the earth into a virtual paradise for all people living then, where animals and humans will live in complete peace where no more animals will eat each other, as the wolf will lie down with a lamb, and a lion will eat straw like the ox. There will be no more wars or sicknesses. Then Jesus will turn the paradise earth over to God so that God may be all things to everyone. First Corinthians 15:25–28 and Revelation 21:1–4 give us the promise!

PLANET EARTH IS GOD'S GARDEN FOR PERFECTING SOULS (1 CORINTHIAN 3:6-9)

The supreme ruler of all things, including all the separate universes has been busy creating perfected and tested spirit beings as well as giving human souls the opportunity to follow in Jesus footsteps in order to be a part of the chosen ones that will make up the great crowd who come out of the great tribulation, as shown in the book of Matthew 24:3–31 and 25:31–40 and Revelation 7:9, 10, 14, 15. The spiritual sons that God has been selecting from mankind are those humans who have proven themselves faithful to God and have accepted Jesus as their King and Savior from God and are to become the future Kings over the new earth. Jesus has referred to these ones as his little flock who are to inherit the kingdom of heaven as in Luke 10:20 and 12: 32–34, so these are the spiritual sons of God that the Bible says about them in Hebrews 3:1–4 who have the heavenly calling! The other ones, referred to as a great crowd of mankind, are the ones who have the hope of living in a paradise earth under the protection of the heavenly kings where they will live long, peaceful lives, as long as trees, for thousands of years.

Jesus was the first tested, perfect person of the human family, as Hebrews 2:10 states, he was to be the first one of many future brothers who were to be tested, as Jesus had been and to become his spiritual brothers in the heavenly part of God's kingdom as 1 Corinthians 15:20–23 and 44–58 states regarding these spiritual brothers of Jesus who are to rule over the whole earth.

The rest of mankind are in the continuing process of working toward a state of perfection as both Adam and Eve were in the beginning. and once these ones have been perfected and have undergone the final test of their perfection because they will have to pass the final test as recorded in Revelation 20:7–9, as this shows the Devil is allowed out of his prison to once again try to turn these now perfected human souls away from trusting in God, and to follow him in his rebellion against the rulership of God and His Christ and the other one hundred forty-four thousand spirit brothers of Jesus.

THE THREE INVISIBLE FORCES THAT OPERATE IN THE PHYSICAL UNIVERSE (THAT INVISIBLE FORCE OF GRAVITY)

Let us examine in detail each of these invisible forces of energy that control all things in the physical world. Without these forces, this physical world could not exist. For example, let us examine the invisible force called GRAVITY. What is this powerful force, and how does it affect the visible world? Most people know it exists because they see that all physical things fall down toward the earth and never up or sideways, so the earth itself must have a lot to do with this invisible force, doesn't it? So what exactly is it, and why does it have such a big effect on everything on earth where it seems to act like a powerful magnet?

The earth itself does, in fact, act like a giant magnet, but why and how does it work? Gravity works in electromagnetic waves of heated electrons that are attracted to other particles of similar components. Looking at the earth and its iron core that is heated to some thousands of degrees Fahrenheit, one can see that this would create a tremendous attraction of waves of electrons shooting to the surface that would attract like components—that is what all people and animals are composed of—just as the Bible states in Genesis 2:7 that man is made of the dust of the earth.

We can see why there is such a powerful attraction; all things are made of similar properties, but that is not the only attraction, as we need to know exactly what is in the dust of the earth, what are the main properties that are magnetic so that it has this powerful attraction, what is the main thing that is attracted to a magnet. It is the iron element that is the most powerful, isn't it? And that is the real force—electromagnetism that binds all humans and the animal creation to the earth. Mass attracts mass that is of the same basic structure of components!

The earth has an abundance of iron together with its center iron core, plus an exceptional electromagnetic field that covers the entire earth from one pole to the other pole that is also a very powerful protective force that circles the entire globe that is absolutely essential for all life on this planet. Which now takes us to our next subject—that wonderful other invisible force called ELECTRICITY!

THE INVISIBLE FORCE OF ELECTRICITY THAT RUNS THE MODERN WORLD

Let us examine in detail that elusive and invisible force that is absolutely essential to this modern world for almost everything that mankind depends on in today's modern way of life. Without which, hardly any of today's conveniences would continue to operate, such as planes, trains, buses, trucks, cars, and ships that carry everything from humans and products and the foods that humans need to continue to survive in this modern world. Not to mention their homes like lights, heating, etc., that are all run by electricity. And what about your cell phones, TVs, radios, computers, and the Internet? All dependent on electricity. If you have ever had your power off, you can certainly appreciate how valuable this source of power is.

It has proven to be one of the most precious gifts that God has ever provided for all mankind, and mankind is gradually realizing that the creator of this whole world has provided all the things necessary to create this wonderful invisible force by all the natural means, such as wind power, wave power, solar power. All of these means have always been available. However, until just recently, mankind has been using the most polluting means of power. Dirty coal and oil have been responsible for causing global warming and polluting the air, the land, and the water, which is causing many serious illnesses such as cancer, heart attacks, and strokes, just to mention a few. Also, this includes fierce storms, floods, hurricanes, and tornadoes that seem to be getting worse.

This modern world has many reasons to appreciate the wonderful power source of electricity because it is such a clean source of power and the very easiest to create and to store in batteries aw well. Car producers are finally starting to create the right type of vehicles, and governments are finally getting on the bandwagon by starting to get serious about creating these electrical places for people to plug in and recharge their vehicles, much like what happened with all the gas stations of times past when cars first started to replace the horse and buggy. Let's help them today by doing our part and change from those old oil and gas polluters to the new horse and buggies that are fueled by that clean energy of . . . ELECTRICITY.

THAT INVISIBLE FORCE CALLED THE WIND THAT CONTROLS THE WEATHER

That elusive force that is known as the WIND that no one can know where it comes from or where it goes in its many travels around the earth, but we can certainly appreciate that it is a very real force that can create tremendous problems on this planet, such as hurricanes and tornadoes which seem to be getting more ferocious and dangerous every year. And yet we know that this planet with all its vegetation and greenery could not exist without the wind that brings the clouds and the rain and controls everything that happens on this planet.

The wind is also another gift from the creator in so many ways. Just look at the many beautiful birds as they soar through the sky on the wings of the wind and also the scent of freshly cut grass as the wind brings it to your sense of smell or the fragrance of a beautiful rose—all these things are because of the wind and its power over everything on earth. Look how boaters with sail boats enjoy the wind in their sails, all without any cost. It's free. Another gift from a loving creator.

The wind is also such a joy for all those people who love water surfing too, not to mention all those people who love flying on the wind, whether in a private plane or on a commercial jetliner. Just imagine if there were no planes in the skies, people would be back to having to travel for vast distances by trains or by bus or private cars, as it was in times past before planes were invented. So once again, what a wonderful gift from a loving God is the wind for mankind to enjoy in so many ways that would be impossible if it were not for the wind.

The wind, like both gravity and electricity, has been and continues to be a real joy and an absolute necessity for life, as we know it on this beautiful planet, the only place in the galaxy that is suitable for life as far as we can determine at the present time. So mankind needs to really appreciate this powerful and invisible force that continues to make life both interesting as the main controller of the ever-changing weather. Also, the many things that can only be enjoyed by the use of the wind such as wind surfing or surfing on the waves of the sea, and all those beautiful and ever-changing sunsets created by the wind!

ALL THINGS IN THIS PHYSICAL UNIVERSE COME IN THREES

From the creator of all the universes to the very smallest part of the atoms of all physical things in this physical universe, we find that everything is made of three separate primary components. The best place to start and show how this is in fact what is true in all things, let us start with the creator himself. How does this apply to God? The Bible indicates to us that God is a trinity of three separate entities that make up one God, as GOD the Father, GOD the Son, and GOD the Holy Spirit. These three entities make up ONE SUPREME GOD!

Next, let us now look at man who the Bible says was made in God's image. What does that mean in his image? The Bible gives us the answer where it shows us that man is also made of three separate parts, namely SPIRIT, MIND, and BODY that equals ONE HUMAN SOUL!

Next, let us examine the common atom. How many primary parts are in the atom? There are three again: the proton, the neutron, and the electron. And look at a chicken's egg three parts again: the shell, the white, and the yoke, but just one egg. Next, let us look at water. How many parts again? It's H20, and it can also be put into three separate parts: a gas, a solid, and a liquid. Again, we see all things come in threes!

And just as there are the three separate universes that we have shown in the first part of this book, these three universes also have three main parts to each of them. Let us look at the chief one first where the Bible shows this in Paul's writings in 2 Corinthians 12:1–4 where Paul says that he was caught away to the third heaven which in turn would suggest there are at least three separate heavens too!

Now what about the physical universe where we are? Are there three separate parts to this universe too? Let us see. There are the physical galaxies and their stars and planets, moons, etc., together with asteroids and comets that make up only less than 5 percent. Then there is that dark energy that comprises of about 70 percent of the known universe that science now suspects controls the physical universe that is visible to human eyes. And then there is what they call dark matter, about another 25 percent of the known universe that is also unseen to human eyes! So once again, we see that all things, including the physical universe, consist of three distinct parts!

SEEMING CONTRADICTIONS IN THE WORD OF GOD

As an example in 1 Corinthians 15:50, it states that flesh and blood, in other words human beings, cannot inherit the kingdom of God in heaven. And yet in still other texts in the Bible, such as Luke 12:32, it shows Jesus telling certain ones of his little group of his followers that they are to inherit the kingdom, as in Matthew 25:34 where he says, "Come and inherit the kingdom." What a seeming contradiction this must seem to be, and especially to all those Christians in the many different persuasions who believe and are told by their particular group that if they remain in good standing, their hope is to go to heaven and inherit that kingdom of God. So what is the answer to this seeming contradiction?

First, we need to see just who Jesus was talking to when he made these promises. According to that text in Luke, Jesus refers to them as a little flock. In other words, a small special group who are to inherit the kingdom of God where we discover in the book of Revelation 14:1–3 that there number is just one hundred forty-four thousand and who have been bought from the earth to be made kings as Revelation 5:9 and 10 states. These are the ones referred to in the book of Hebrews 3:1 who have the "heavenly hope." Then in 1 Corinthians 15:51–57, it shows that these ones must be changed from human souls to immortal spirits like Jesus was when resurrected, as it is this that was once human of flesh and blood must now be changed into spirit bodies.

So what seemed to be a contradiction in the Bible can easily be explained as truth when one is willing to do a little research into any subject, but it requires a little effort on anyone's part in his search for truth. So we have learned so far as to who the little flock is, as they are said to be kings and are to rule over the earth. Who are they to rule over should be our next question. How do we see just exactly who these ones are?

From here, we need to go to yet another part of the Bible that answers this question for us. Psalms 37:11 and 29 that tells us who they are; they are the MEEK who are to inherit the earthly paradise, the one hundred forty-four thousand kings along with the KING of kings, Jesus, are the rulers over. So again, with a little effort, everything in the Bible can be explained as truth. Just as the Bible says in John 17:3, how important it is to know the truth about God, and if you were to ask God, that knowledge will be given to you! See John 16:23.

MORE SEEMING CONTRADICTIONS IN THE BIBLE

Still another scripture text that seems to be a contradiction is in Luke 23:43 that sees Jesus telling the thief that was crucified beside him, "Truly I tell you, today, you will be with me in paradise." But how could that be possible when Jesus was to be dead in hell for three days, as Acts 2:31, 32 states? John 2:19–21, as well as Luke 24:7, all contradict this. So how do we clarify this seeming contradiction? For one thing, we need to realize that the Bible, in its original language, did not have punctuation marks, so the translators would put them in as they saw fit. But notice what happens in the text at Luke 23:43, when we change the coma from where it is in the King James Bible to this: "Truly I tell you today, you will be with me in paradise." Notice that Jesus is just telling him that day that the thief would be with Jesus in paradise but not that same day. Otherwise, you make the Bible contradict common sense. Jesus certainly was not suggesting that hell was in any way to be associated with paradise. Also, there are many other texts in the Bible that tell us when, in the future, that the earth will be a paradise.

So what seemed to be a contradiction in the Bible can easily be explained as truth when one is willing to do a little research into the particular subject, and then it can be made clear that the Bible does not contradict itself, but many times seems to because of translation problems, such as the one in Luke 23:43.

Still, another text causes a serious problem for many Christians, and that would seem to go against God's command to mankind to be fruitful and fill the earth with your progeny. The text in question here is found in

Matthew 22:30 where Jesus is asked a question about those who are to be resurrected from the dead and whose wife would this lady be because she had been married several times and had several different husbands. Notice carefully what Jesus says to these religious leaders in Luke 20:34–36. He states, "Those who are" counted worthy "of that system of things and the resurrection of the dead do not marry, and are like the angels, neither can they die anymore." The secret to understand this text and the answer that Jesus gave is in the words *counted worthy*. The last book in the Bible, Revelation 20:4 and 6, shows that these are the spiritual sons of God by means of the first resurrection and are to be the kings of the new earth.

THE RELIGION OF MORMONISM

(ORIGINALLY A POLYGAMIST SOCIETY)

This is yet another cultlike religion that originated with an old idea of polygamy that was first mentioned in the Bible in the book of Genesis where it states that some of God's spirit angels rebelled against God's way of doing things and materialized into human forms and took wives for themselves, all whom they chose and continued to have sexual relations with human women and produced a race of giant creatures that terrorized the human race as well as forcing them to help them build many of the giant things that are seen all over the earth, such as Stonehenge and the giant statues on Easter Island and many other structures all over the planet (See Genesis 6:1–4). Polygamy began with these rebels against the true God's plans for the human race!

One can see the similarity in the beginning of Mormonism, which again tried to restart what these rebellious angels did in the time of Noah, and one can see how the true GOD felt about this in the book of Genesis 6:5–7, 11, and 17. The archenemy of the true GOD is none other than Satan, the Devil, who continues to pretend to be an angel of enlightenment in order to turn people away from the true God by getting them to disobey the commandments of GOD. See 2 Corinthians 11:14, 15 and Job 38:4 and 7. One only needs to look at how many wives God gave to Adam. *Just ONE!*

In the books of Enoch, which were left out of the Bible, it states that there were some two hundred angels who left their proper place in the spirit world and entered the physical world of mankind to pollute the human race by creating these hybrids, as the Bible refers to them as the giants of old, some with six fingers and six toes on their hands and feet and two rows of teeth. Some are fifteen to eighteen feet tall giants. See the following texts in the Bible in Jude 6; 2 Peter 2:4, 5; 1 Peter 3:19 and 20; Deuteronomy 3:11; 1:28; 2:10, 11, 21; and Numbers 13:31–33. The Bible shows in many places why God destroyed the people in these lands, such as at Deuteronomy 12:28–31.

THE RELIGION OF THE SEVENTH-DAY ADVENTISTS

This man-made religion is yet another one of Satan's means of dividing the people of earth into believing yet one more belief system and to create doubts in the minds of people as to what or where the real truth is? Every thinking person must begin to question his or her faith when they see all the division among those professing to believe in the very same Bible.

One must wonder: how can there be such division among all these different persuasions of Christianity when they all profess to believe in the very same book, the Holy Bible? Also, they all claim to believe in the words of Jesus Christ.

How is it possible that so many people can read the very same book and yet cannot agree on what it says? For example, let us look at the belief of the Seventh-Day Adventists that their leaders have claimed that is essential, namely the Sabbath day, and that Christians must keep it holy and not to do any work on that day. Is this true? Were Christians ever given such an order by Christ? Let us examine what the Bible says about this subject.

To begin with, we see the exact opposite in Jesus's own actions on the Sabbath as written in Matthew 12:1–15 where he spent the time curing all the many people who came to him to be cured of their many illnesses. Jesus did a lot of work on the Sabbath to show Israel that it was no longer to be enforced.

He purposely did this to show the people why the Sabbath was given to Israel and that he had come to free them from the old covenant given to them through Moses, with its many decrees that convicted them of being sinners and in need of a Savior to free them from the curse of the law of decrees, which included the Sabbath law (Galatians 3:18–25; 9–11). Jesus never once asked his followers to keep the Sabbath law!

THE VERY REAL DANGER TO ALL THE FOLLOWERS OF THE SEVENTH-DAY ADVENTISTS

The leaders of this man-made religion have separated all their followers from the promise of God that was made to Abraham, where it was to be through his seed that all nations of the earth would be blessed, which this seed turned out to be Jesus, the Christ of Almighty God. It would ONLY be because of all people of those nations who were willing to put their faith in the ransom sacrifice that Jesus provided on the torture stake at Calvary where he nailed the law of decrees and did away with the curse because it is written, "Cursed is everyone who is nailed to a stake." (See Colossians 2:13–17, 20; Galatians 3:16–18; Galatians 4:4, 5, 9–11; Romans 10:4; and 2 Corinthians 3:14.

The covenant made with the nation of Israel that contained the Ten Commandments and included the Sabbath law was given some four hundred fifty years after the promise of God to Abraham, which was to be a far better second covenant that included the blood, not of bulls or goats but rather the blood of Jesus Christ, the Lamb of God. (See Hebrews 8:6–13; 9:12–28 and Ephesians 2:15.)

The whole purpose of the law that was given to the nation of Israel was to show them that they were sinners and in need of a savior, and so the law was to be a tutor leading them to Christ Jesus. See Galatians 3:18–26, 29, 4:4–11, 5:1–4 and 3:2, 6, 9–13. All these texts make it very plain that Christians today are no longer obligated to keep this old law.

The Sabbath law that was given to the people of ancient Israel and which included the law of decrees can be seen as done away with by the letters quoted above. Everyone should be able to see the danger of this belief in forcing followers of today in keeping this old law that actually separates one from the promise to Abraham that Jesus was to be the mediator of the new and better covenant that would free them from the old covenant of decrees. See Galatians 5:4 along with all the quotes above that make this abundantly clear!

ALL THE ABOVE QUOTES FROM THE BIBLE SHOW THE REAL DANGER OF BEING SEPARATED FROM JESUS AND THE PROMISE TO ABRAHAM

JEHOVAH'S CHRISTIAN WITNESSES

This is yet another man-made religion that came into being near the end of the 19th century that was designed around the idea that the present system of things was about to end, and that God was about to bring about the promise in the Bible of the Kingdom of God being established on the earth, and the millennium rule by Jesus Christ to begin, along with the complete destruction of the present system of things including all false religions and national governments who are ruining the earth. See Revelation 11:18, and Matthew 24:3-47. They believe that God has chosen them to warn the world of the end.

Could this all be the real truth? and that they really are the only religion in the modern world who are doing the will of God, and warning the world of the impending destruction of the present system of things. How can we know if this is true? What does the Bible say about how to recognize the true faith of the followers of Jesus Christ? Let us look at Jesus words on this subject. In Matthew 28:18-20, Jesus tells all of his followers to go and make disciples of others, teaching them to obey all the things I have commanded you. Are Jehovah's christian witnesses obeying this command of Jesus? We have to answer YES, and are they busy at preaching about the Kingdom of God? The answer again is YES, and it would appear that they are the only ones who are doing the will of God in this respect. We never hear the ministers in the churchs of christendom or their followers doing what Jesus commanded his followers to do, as we see individual witnesses doing in their preaching about the Kingdom of God, and warning mankind of the end of this world.

Another very important thing to look for, how to recognize Jesus true followers was that they were to be separate from the world in that they would not go along with the immoral practises of the modern world, in such things as the many national wars, same sex marriages, homosexuality, etc. which are all condemned in the Bible as in Romans 1:18-32 and see also John 17:11-26. Anyone who is familiar with the teachings of Jehovah 's Christian Witnesses will realize immediately that all of the above is true regarding this faith, as the witnesses do not vote in elections, nor do they take part in the many wars of the world as they refuse military service, although they obey all the laws of the governments that do not conflict with the laws of God. They pay taxes just like all the rest of us, and are usually good law-abiding citizens, and just as the early christians did, they engage in House to House preaching us early christians did also, as in Acts 5;27-42. Very interesting parallels!

THE MANY BELIEF SYSTEMS OF THE CHURCHES OF CHRISTENDOM HAVE FAILED JESUS AND MANKIND

When one looks at the many different persuasions of so-called Christian churches, it is very obvious that these religions have not produced in their followers the zeal to preach to others about the hope of salvation that they are said to believe in. How unlike this is to the early Christians who fearlessly preached about Jesus to everyone and many times at the very cost of their lives. Christians today, in most of the world, do not have any fears about doing the same thing in preaching to others about faith in Jesus Christ and the good news that Jesus told his followers to preach to everyone all over the earth. See Acts 5:27–42; 7:54–60 and Matthew 28:18–20.

Do you know of any of the followers of your particular faith who are busy doing the things that Jesus told all his followers to be doing, in preaching to others about their faith in Christ Jesus, and about the good news of the kingdom of God? I have not personally heard of even one in today's world doing what Jesus said would mark them as his true followers other than the Christian Witnesses of Jehovah who have come to my door on numerous occasions in the past. May they be the one true faith in the world today? They are seen to be doing all the things that the Bible states about true Christians and their being no part of this world, and all its wars where they have refused to be a part of the armies of this old world where so-called Christians on both sides of their many wars go about killing each other, even though they are all supposed to be followers of the prince of peace, Jesus. What hypocrisy this seems to be.

It is a very real danger for any person to leave their eternal life up to someone else, like so many people do, who attend their different church or synagogue. What if they are not telling you the truth about God and his requirements for eternal life? This is why Jesus states in John 17:3 the necessity for everyone to take in accurate knowledge about God and Jesus Christ and then to apply that information in your daily lives so as to be found doing the "will of God" and telling others the good news about Jesus and the sure hope that all Christians have of eternal life!

THE ISLAM RELIGION

Created by MUHAMMAD, Founder and Prophet of Islam and His Revelations in the Koran (or Qur'an) and the Sunna

Another man-made religion that was started on a false premise by the same enemy of the true GOD, Satan, the Devil, who continues to deceive mankind into doing the things that are detestable to the true GOD, Yahweh! For example, the demands of their followers to be forced to call to prayer five times a day and to bow down to the earth, facing Mecca. Doing this is exactly what Satan asked Jesus to do to bow down to him, and he would make him ruler of all the kingdoms of the world as recorded in the book of Matthew 4:8, 9. Notice Jesus's answer to the Devil, where he tells him to go away, for it is written, "You must worship ONLY Yahweh, the Almighty GOD and bow down to no one on earth."

One can see the similarity when we see what Jesus said back to the Devil and how GOD feels about bowing down to false gods such as Satan, The Devil, the great opposer of the true GOD! It is interesting to note that the true GOD never demands that mankind must bow down to him, but only false gods demand such allegiance from their poor, misguided followers.

See Job 38:3 and 7. Rather, the true GOD asks man to stand up like a man and not to bow down to anyone, as man was created in the image of GOD.

How superior are the laws of the true GOD, such as "Thou shalt not kill" and "Love thy enemies," "Pray for others as you would have them do for you," "Do unto others as you would have them do unto you." Compare these laws with the actions of the poor, misguided souls under the influence of the ISIL group and others of the same mind-set who Satan is using to do his bidding of torturing, killing, and enslaving everyone under their control by turning people against one another so as to destroy all mankind if possible. Satan knows that his time is running out for ruining the earth and mankind. He has convinced his followers that they are actually fulfilling a prophecy in the Bible in Matthew 24:20–22 about a great tribulation that is to lead to the great last war of Armageddon that is mentioned in Revelation 16:14–16.

THE MANY RELIGIONS OF EAST INDIA AND PAKISTAN

There are so many man-made beliefs in these countries with differing religions that has caused such divisions among the majority of their people. In this respect, it is similar to the many different sects of the Christian religions, all divided and all following their own particular brand of beliefs that again shows the Devil's handiwork of dividing people and causing the many conflicts in all parts of the world today.

By creating all these separate sects and belief systems, Satan has been able to manipulate the people of the earth to do his bidding, which is totally contrary to the decrees of the true God of the universe, Yahweh who had declared in the very beginning that mankind was to subdue all the earth and to make it into a worldwide paradise for all the human race to enjoy, just as the Garden of Eden was. Instead, Satan has had mankind build large cities and all clump together, which has created crime and violence and pollution on a worldwide scale, not to mention ruining the entire planet by causing people of the many different belief systems to continue to fight one another because of religion.

The problem with all these belief systems, other than the so-called Christian ones, is the same one, namely, that they do not offer a means of salvation to their followers and a way out from sin and its penalty of death. Please look up and read the following texts from the Bible and learn why it is so important to know what the real truth is about the only way to GOD: Romans 2:11–16 and Romans 6:23 and 3:22–26. Satan, the Devil, does not care what you believe so long as you do not put any faith in the Almighty God's ONLY means of salvation that is through faith in JESUS CHRIST. Please read what the Bible says about this in Acts 4:10–12; 3:13–15; and John 14:6–11.

THE BUDDHISM RELIGION

The Doctrine Attributed to Gautama Buddha

This is yet one more man-made religion that is one of the major beliefs of the Chinese and Indian people as well as many others in all parts of the world that was created by the great enemy of the truth and the God of Truth, Jesus Christ. The real danger to all the followers of this religion is that they are parted from belief in the only way to eternal life through the one and only means of salvation—that is, by means of faith in Jesus, the Christ of Almighty God. See Acts 4:10–12, as this plainly states that there is no other name in heaven or on earth that can save anyone from death and is also able to grant eternal life to all those who put faith in his name.

One needs to recognize that all people on earth are imperfect and that any honest person will admit to this simple truth, will be honest with themselves, and will acknowledge as the Bible says, will make them sinners, as they have missed the mark of perfection which is what imperfect means, and so are constituted as sinners with its penalty which is death. See Romans 6:23 and John 8:23–30.

Satan, the great enemy of truth, does not care what you believe in, so long as you do not believe in God's ONLY WAY of salvation, as Romans 3:10–29 and 5:8–21 shows. So to all of you followers of this man-made religion,

God's plan of eternal life is ONLY through JESUS and not through any other way, as so many of you have been led to believe!

Please read these following texts in the Bible, starting with Matthew 7:13, 14 and 21–23; and Romans 2:11–16; 10:2–4, and 10:9–15.

The Holy Bible is the ONLY BOOK that promises the GIFT of ETERNAL LIFE to all people who accept the ALMIGHTY GOD's means of salvation—that is, JESUS, the LAMB OF GOD, who alone came to this planet to show mankind how they should live their lives and to love one another and then provided the "ransom price" by sacrificing his right to life on the torture stake at Calvary in order to acquire the authority of God to adopt all mankind who accept Jesus as their personal Savior.

"BUDDHISM IS NOT THE WAY"

Many people around the world have been led to believe that there are many paths all leading to God and or heavenly bliss, which is just the same as believing in the erroneous theory of evolution that believes that intelligent mankind came from monkeys that has no basis in fact, nor one iota of proof other than pretty pictures painted and dreamed up by some paid artist.

Unlike Buddha, who never claimed to have died for you or anyone else, Jesus, on the other hand, did just that and further claimed that he was the only way to God, the Father, and the gateway to eternal life. Here are his exact words on the subject in John 14:6: "I am the Way, the truth, and the life. No one comes to the Father except through me." See also John 17:1–5 and Isaiah 45:18–22.

So the question one needs to ask is this: Do you value the truth, or are you not concerned about truth and are just willing to go along with a lie because it may be convenient to believe it? You may do just that, as you are a free moral agent, but this thinking will not lead you to any heavenly bliss or the eternal life that you might be hoping to attain to. THINK AGAIN! Please read John 8:31–36 and 42–44 and John 12:35–50!

The conclusion of the matter regarding all these man-made religions should be to question first their inception as to who started the religion and what are the real beliefs and what was the basis for the tenets. Do they help mankind in general to live better lives? Do any of them promise eternal life?

NEXT COMES THE RESTORATION OF PLANET EARTH TO A PARADISE CONDITION

This restoring of the earth on an earth-wide scale is the original command of Almighty God to the first inhabitants of earth in the Garden of Eden, namely to be fruitful and to multiply and subdue the earth and make it into a paradise, as I have shown you how to accomplish this in the Garden of Eden! I will continue to assist you in this task as you enjoy living in an earthly paradise.

This is what Jesus and his associate rulers will now take on as they help mankind fulfill God's original purpose for the earth. In the next sequence of events, we come to the end of this period of the one-thousand-year reign, during which time the whole earth would have been restored to a virtual paradise with all humans having been brought to a perfect condition. But as yet not having been tested, we see Satan being released from the abyss to once more being allowed to try and turn people away from God. These are shown to be as the sand in the sea or numberless unknown.

In this next sequence, we see the Devil and all those who follow him are destroyed by being thrown into the lake of fire. This symbolizes their final and total destruction (Revelation 20:10). Then comes the great white throne judgment, the final judgment of all those in death and Hades or the common grave of all mankind, including the sea and all those dead in it. And they are to be judged according to the things written in the scrolls, as to all their deeds during their lives on earth. Anyone who does not have their name written in the scroll of life is to be hurled into the lake of fire where both the wild beast and the Devil already are. This symbolizes their eternal destruction!

Next, we see the final promise of God to become fulfilled in this final sequence where all those whose names are in the scroll of life are granted to go to the tree of life and live forever, as in Revelation 21:1–4, 7, 22:1 and 2. These are the ones who have the hope of living forever in a paradise earth as Psalms 37:11, 29 states about these very ones that are seen in Revelation 21:1–4.

THE CONCLUSION OF THIS BOOK IS TO EXPLAIN THE FUTURE ACCORDING TO THE WORD OF GOD

We have outlined just briefly all the occurrences that lead up to this moment in time and now what is to happen to all the inhabitants of the earth and all other things that exist upon it and out into the far distant future for all those who LOVE GOD!

In the book of Revelation, in chapters 20 and 21, the Bible outlines the sequence of events that are to take place in relation to GOD and the entire human race as well as the Devil being taken from the earth and cast into the abyss so that he is not able to mislead the nations anymore until the one thousand years are ended.

We see also those who have been bought from the earth who are to rule over the new earth and just how many of these who have been bought from among mankind in these texts in Revelation 5:9, 10; 14:1–3; and 20:4 and 6. The number of these is one hundred forty-four thousand that includes the twelve apostles of the Lamb of GOD. They, like the Lord Jesus, have now become spirit beings as 1 Corinthians 15:44, 45 shows, as well as in verses 50–54 and 1 Thessalonians 4:15–17.

The first operation of these new rulers is to rid the earth of all the present governments who have been guilty of ruining the earth under the influence of the invisible ruler of this old world as the following texts make clear in Revelation 11:18; 12:7–12; 20 1–3; and Ephesians 6:12; Psalms 2:1–9; and Jeremiah 25:30–33.

This invisible ruler is none other than Satan, the Devil, who has been the real problem behind all the troubles caused on earth for the past some six thousand years of recorded history and is the real reason why the earth and its people today are in such turmoil. It is because Satan knows his time is about to end, and God's kingdom is about to take over the rulership of all the earth under Christ Jesus, God's appointed King of kings. See Revelation 12:12.

NEXT: WE GO FURTHER INTO THE FUTURE OF THE PLANS OF GOD

In my Father's house (the universe), there are many mansions according to Jesus's words to his disciples, John 14:1–4, and I am going away to prepare places for all of you, as well as all others who follow and have faith in me and the promises of God.

The spirit of the Lord has indicated to mankind a glimpse of the future plans of God for all those who love God. See these texts in 1 Corinthians 2:9, 10; 3:16, 17; and 6:19, 20. Think about the first human beings, Adam and Eve, and their future prospects. Had they remained faithful to their creator and to be the progenitors of the entire human race in an earthly paradise with unending life in perfection with no sickness or disease and with future potential of populating the entire visible universe with their own progeny? This was and is the purpose of Almighty God.

The infinite God does not create things that are not for his purpose. Mankind today, with their farseeing telescopes, can see no end to this vast universe involving billions of galaxies that contain more than a billion individual star systems, their planets and moons.

This continuing creation has no end and is eternal as the creator of all, the Almighty God is, as the Bible states in Isaiah 40:22, 26 as well as Isaiah 45:12, 18, 22 and 1 Timothy 6:16.

The purpose of God is life eternal with an abundance of living things all praising and giving glory to the eternal God, Yahweh. One can just imagine the future of all those individual humans who have been tested and proven worthy of eternal life and now may be given the opportunity to have their very own planet to govern and to populate an entire new planet with their very own progeny, just as God had granted to Adam and Eve. This is just giving mankind a brief glimpse into the future plans of God and his ever-expanding universe without end. (Room for all!)

THE GREAT HONOUR AND OBLIGATION OF ALL CHRISTIANS

Most of mankind do not realize what a great Honour it is to be called as children of The Almight God , and ambassadors for GOD to the whole world of mankind, sharing with them All of The "Good News" about the coming Kingdom Of GOD, and what that means to all of the human race. It is the answer to The "Lord's Prayer" in Matthew 6:10 that Christians have been praying for, for some 2000 years ever since Jesus was on earth.

It is such Good News, that they have to share with all of mankind, how could one not want to share it with everyone who will listen ? Please see the following texts at Romans 10:9-15, Matthew 24:14; 28:18-20. We see from those texts the obligation on each follower of Christ, that we as individuals are obligated to go and make disciples of others, teaching them all of the things that Jesus asked his followers to do, and to show Love to everyone and especially to those who are Real true Followers of Jesus.

In following the footsteps of Christ Jesus, all true Believers must be separate from this old world that is alienated from God, as the rule of the present systems of things is Satan, The Devil, the great enemy of all that is Good. Notice Jesus words about this in John 17:14-20; 1st John 5:19 and 1st. Peter 2:21;3:15-17;4:3-9, also James 4:4,7-10 ; James 1:19-25

Unlike the many different preachers in the many different churches of the sects of Christendom, who are all divided against each other by their own interpretations from the very same Bible, True Christians are not in such disarray, but are busy doing the will of God and helping all others who are willing to listen to do the same. The religions of both Catholic and Protestant belief systems have obviously failed to engender in their own people the desire to do the "Will of God', and this is why one never hears any individuals of these many different religions speaking about God and The "Good News" of The Kingdom, and the salvation thru Jesus Christ. There seems to be only one group of people on this earth who are seen to be doing The "Will of God" and preaching to others about the Good news of The Kingdom to all who listen, and who have kept themselves as separate from the world as Jesus stated about his true followers.

THE END

WE WISH TO ADD THE FOLLOWING EXPLANATIONS TO THE ENTIRE HUMAN FAMILY OF PLANET EARTH

The final conclusion of this extraordinary book is to show the people the "real truth" about why the world is the way it is and why God has allowed all mankind the many means of governing themselves and to go on for so long a period of time with no interference from God.

There has been a multipurpose behind this long period of time in order for God to carry out his purposes and to allow the three separate universes to experience what it is like to have free will and to exercise that will and to make choices and then to see the consequences of their actions.

This long period of time has also allowed individual humans to exercise this same freedom in each generation throughout the ages and to make choices with this free will and to see the consequences of those choices.

It has also allowed God the opportunity to choose special humans who have demonstrated the qualities that God has seen in their actions that are what he wanted to see for those who he has chosen to be kings along with his only begotten Son to rule over the new earth that is to come!

We welcome all the people
Of this world who are
Sincerely interested
In helping the poor
And in knowing more about
The future of planet earth
To write us at brothersofjesusministry@gmail.com

ATTENTION: To all of you who purchase this extraordinary book, you will not be the only ones who will benefit, as most of royalties from this book are for helping the very poor, especially those children of the world who need help in many of the poor areas of the different countries. When you help the poor, you are really lending to God, and God will repay you in kind! (It is as you have done it unto me. Matthew 25:40)

www.ingramcontent.com/pod-product-compliance
Lightning Source LLC
LaVergne TN
LVHW020425080526
838202LV00055B/5037